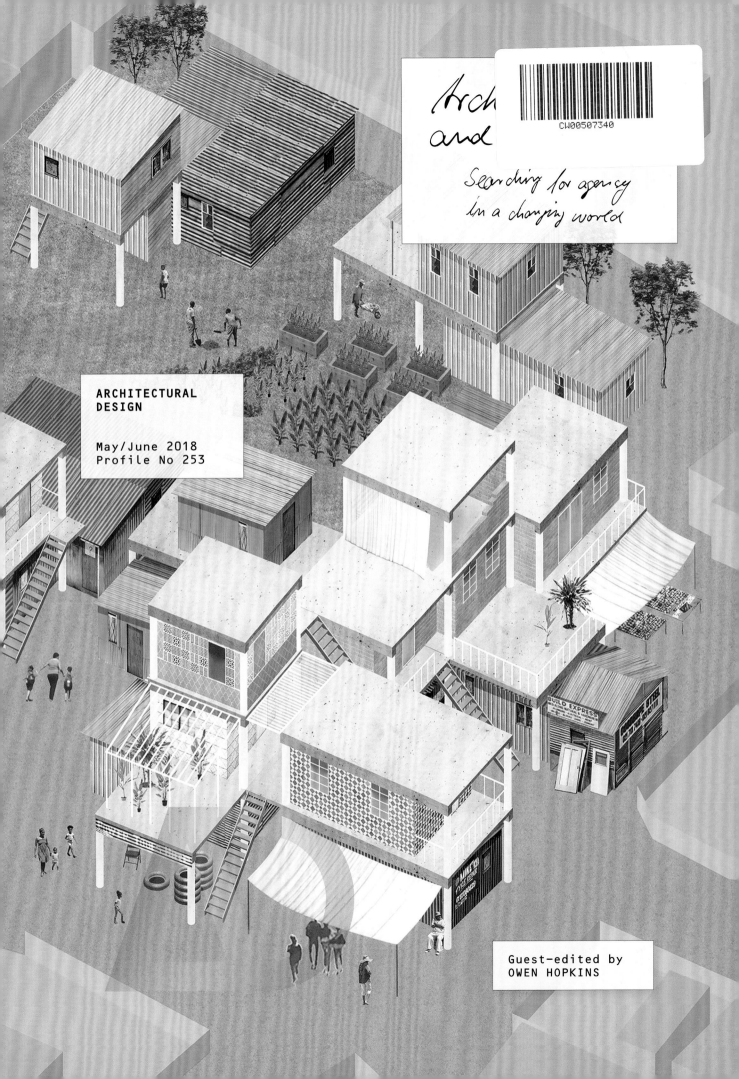

Arch
and

Searching for agency
in a changing world

CW00507340

ARCHITECTURAL
DESIGN

May/June 2018
Profile No 253

BUILD EXPRESS

Guest-edited by
OWEN HOPKINS

ISSN 0003-8504
ISBN 978 1119 332633

Editorial Offices
John Wiley & Sons
9600 Garsington Road
Oxford
OX4 2DQ

T +44 (0)1865 776868

Consultant Editor
Helen Castle

Managing Editor
Caroline Ellerby
Caroline Ellerby Publishing

Freelance Contributing Editor
Abigail Grater

Publisher
Paul Sayer

Art Direction + Design
CHK Design:
Christian Küsters

Production Editor
Elizabeth Gongde

Prepress
Artmedia, London

Printed in Italy by Printer
Trento Srl

Journal Customer Services
For ordering information,
claims and any enquiry
concerning your journal
subscription please go to
www.wileycustomerhelp
.com/ask or contact your
nearest office.

Americas
E: cs-journals@wiley.com
T: +1 781 388 8598 or
+1 800 835 6770 (toll free
in the USA & Canada)

**Europe, Middle East
and Africa**
E: cs-journals@wiley.com
T: +44 (0)1865 778315

Asia Pacific
E: cs-journals@wiley.com
T: +65 6511 8000

Japan (for Japanese-
speaking support)
E: cs-japan@wiley.com
T: +65 6511 8010 or 005 316
50 480 (toll-free)

Visit our Online Customer
Help available in 7 languages
at www.wileycustomerhelp
.com/ask

Print ISSN: 0003-8504
Online ISSN: 1554-2769

Prices are for six issues
and include postage and
handling charges. Individual-
rate subscriptions must be
paid by personal cheque or
credit card. Individual-rate
subscriptions may not be
resold or used as library
copies.

All prices are subject to
change without notice.

Identification Statement
Periodicals Postage paid
at Rahway, NJ 07065.
Air freight and mailing in
the USA by Mercury Media
Processing, 1850 Elizabeth
Avenue, Suite C, Rahway,
NJ 07065, USA.

USA Postmaster
Please send address changes
to *Architectural Design*,
John Wiley & Sons Inc.,
c/o The Sheridan Press,
PO Box 465, Hanover,
PA 17331, USA

Rights and Permissions
Requests to the Publisher
should be addressed to:
Permissions Department
John Wiley & Sons Ltd
The Atrium
Southern Gate
Chichester
West Sussex PO19 8SQ
UK

F: +44 (0)1243 770 620
E: Permissions@wiley.com

Subscribe to Δ
Δ is published bimonthly
and is available to purchase
on both a subscription basis
and as individual volumes
at the following prices.

Prices
Individual copies:
£29.99 / US$45.00
Individual issues on
Δ App for iPad:
£9.99 / US$13.99
Mailing fees for print
may apply

Annual Subscription Rates
Student: £90 / US$137
print only
Personal: £136 / US$215
print and iPad access
Institutional: £310 / US$580
print or online
Institutional: £388 / US$725
combined print and online
6-issue subscription on
Δ App for iPad: £44.99 /
US$64.99

Front cover: Alex Scott-
Whitby, Lyra's Shadow,
2015. © Alex Scott-Whitby

Inside front cover: Sarah
Wigglesworth Architects,
Unlocking Pentonville,
London, 2017. © Sarah
Wigglesworth Architects
2018

Page 1: Noero Architects/
Rainer Hehl Bureau, Table
House, Cape Town, 2016.
© Noero Architects

03/2018

Δ ARCHITECTURAL DESIGN

May/June   Profile No.

2018   **253**

MIX
Paper from
responsible sources
FSC® C015829

Owen Hopkins is a writer, historian and curator of architecture. He is Senior Curator of Exhibitions and Education at Sir John Soane's Museum in London. Prior to that he was Architecture Programme Curator at the Royal Academy of Arts. He has a longstanding interest in the interactions between architecture, culture, politics and society, which has fed both his writing and curatorial projects, notably at the Royal Academy of Arts, where he was responsible for a number of initiatives exploring the role of architects in public and cultural life through debates about housing, urban regeneration and the notion of the 'maverick' architect, among other topics. A feature of his work is the way he tackles issues and ideas through a range of formats and media, including exhibitions, events programming, commissions and publications. The theme of this issue of ⌂ emerged from a series of events he organised in autumn 2015.

The exhibitions and projects that he has curated include 'The Return the the Past: Postmodernism in British Architecture' (2018) and 'Adam Nathaniel Furman: The Roman Singularity' (2017), both at the Soane, and 'Origins: A Project by Ordinary Architecture' (2016), 'Urban Jigsaw' (2016), 'Mavericks: Breaking the Mould of British Architecture' (2016), 'Four Visions for the Future of Housing' (2015), '100 Buildings 100 Years: Views of British Architecture Since 1914' (2014) and 'Nicholas Hawksmoor: Architect of the Imagination' (2012), all at the Royal Academy.

He is the author of five books: *Lost Futures: The Disappearing Architecture of Post-War Britain* (RA Publications, 2017), *Mavericks: Breaking the Mould of British Architecture* (RA Publications, 2016), *From the Shadows: The Architecture and Afterlife of Nicholas Hawksmoor* (Reaktion, 2015), *Architectural Styles: A Visual Guide* (Laurence King, 2014) and *Reading Architecture: A Visual Lexicon* (Laurence King, 2012). He is also the editor of a collection of essays: *Sensing Architecture* (RA Publications, 2017).

He is a frequent contributor to the architectural and wider press, his work featuring in publications such as *The Independent*, *Dezeen*, *The Architectural Review*, *Architects' Journal*, *The Herald*, *Burlington Magazine*, *Apollo*, *RA Magazine*, *C20 Magazine*, *Spitalfields Life* and *Building Design*. He regularly sits on 'crit' panels at UK architecture schools, and has judged a number of prizes. He is a frequent lecturer and chair of events and has appeared on national TV and radio. ⌂

Architectu
Paradox of

Der Scutt/Poor, Swanke,
Hayden & Connell,
Trump Tower,
721 Fifth Avenue,
New York City,
1983

No building currently symbolises the paradox of architecture and freedom more obviously than Trump Tower. Built by the property developer and latterly President of the United States – de facto 'leader of the free world' – who claims to represent the interests of the culturally and economically overlooked, Trump Tower is the epitome of ostentatious luxury and self-aggrandisement. Combining offices with 'luxury residences', including Donald Trump's own three-storey penthouse, in the words of the Trump Organisation website: 'Trump Tower is one of New York's most visited attractions since its completion in 1983', featuring a 'magnificent waterfall run[ning] through the Atrium of Trump Tower further enhancing its beauty, with Trump Bar and Trump Grill on its entrance and lower level.'

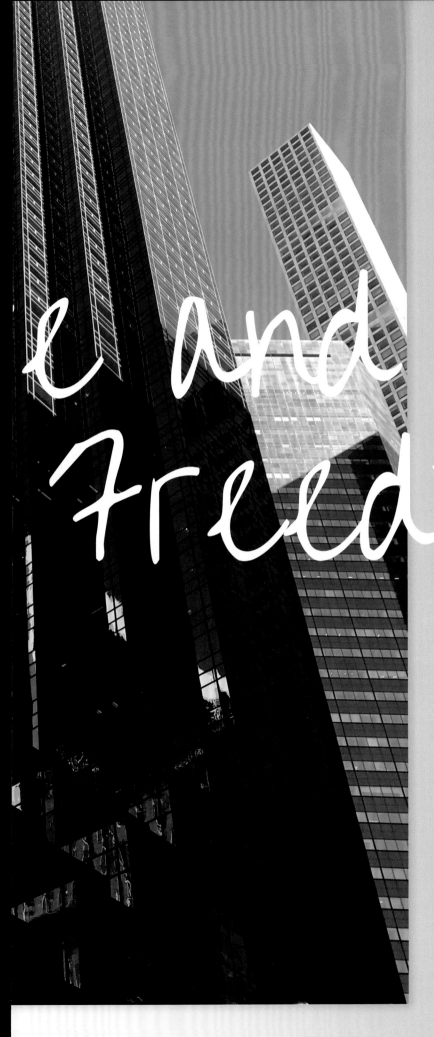

e and the
Freedom

To ask nothing.
To expect nothing.
To depend on nothing.

— Ayn Rand, *The Fountainhead*, 1943[1]

For the Russian-American author Ayn Rand, writing in her famous novel *The Fountainhead*, freedom was about complete self-reliance. Not for her protagonist, the young, ambitious architect Howard Roark, was it enough – indeed even possible – to go with the flow and accept what he saw as the stifling historicist conventions of the architectural establishment. For Roark, his bold Modernist designs were symbols of individual defiance as he embarked on a classic struggle of rugged individualism in the face of the closed ranks of collectivist society and the systems that shape it – or so the story goes.

Since its publication in 1943, *The Fountainhead* has become an important text for libertarians and those who claim to be proponents of total individual liberty. It was even cited as an influence by the property developer turned TV personality Donald Trump in the 2016 US presidential election.[2] Rand's choice of architecture – or specifically the figure of the architect – for the book's motif/protagonist is a consistently intriguing one with, like the political philosophy the book espouses, many contradictions. There is the notion of the sheer force of will of the individual bringing a design into existence; the multiple obstacles therein, whether practical, financial or cultural; the way architecture is perceived as a series of styles or conventions that threaten to subsume individual creativity and innovation. While seductive, all of these ideas are, of course, fictions, or at the very least gross oversimplifications. Of all creative disciplines, architecture is in reality the least libertarian – it has always depended on collaboration, compromise and discussion – and is defined by its constraints: the limits of materials, the effects of gravity, budget, and above all that buildings are functional things. So in a sense, Rand's idea of architecture is a straw man. By the very nature of the discipline, Roark was never going to succeed in achieving complete individual liberty, even in the construction of the skyscraper as a (phallic) symbol of personal (male) achievement, which stands as supposed evidence of his final vindication in the book's closing pages.

Limits and Delimits

If a Randian individual liberty is by definition unobtainable for the architect (let alone everyone else), what of architecture itself? On the most basic level we might see architecture as inherently limiting freedom. Erecting a building or even a simple wall serves to separate and demarcate what was once freely traversable; it is a spatial imposition that physically forces us to alter our route and go around. But what if that wall stands between us and a cliff face to a deep gorge, or is keeping a dangerous animal away? Here, conversely, architecture is creating freedom for everyone: freedom from falling to our deaths or of being gored by an aggressive bull, for instance. In this sense, freedom is not an absolute, but a series of constantly shifting codependencies, which in the case of architecture is about finding a balance between those interventions that limit individual action and those that protect us all – and those that do both. To some extent this balance is present in every work of architecture, but becomes most explicit and with a clear social-political dimension in the idea of prison and of intentional confinement. In these situations, architecture is used to severely limit the freedom of an individual in order to protect the freedom of society.

Yet architecture is, of course, not always about limiting the freedom of the individual for the greater common good. It can create new freedoms for the individual. At root, every building is a shelter that frees its inhabitants from suffering the effects of cold or inclement weather. It also offers some degree of security or protection – both for ourselves and our property. While increasing the freedom of its owner/user, the erection of a building does necessarily result in a decrease in the freedom of society or of the collective: the land is no longer able to be used freely; the materials are no longer able to be used by someone else (or their purchase has reduced supply, thereby increasing the price for others); or some other kind of usually very minor, but sometimes significant, deleterious impact on the common or public realm.

Balancing Freedoms

In this way, we can see architecture as existing in the centre of a series of reciprocal relationships between the freedom of the individual and that of the collective, with the role of the architect at its most fundamental level about trying to find the appropriate balance. It can be argued that this is inherent to the practice of architecture and is consequently manifested to a greater or lesser extent in every project undertaken by architects. We can see how it plays out at various moments over history, both through individual works and collective endeavours assembled over time. The Parthenon (447–432 BC) stands as the defining symbol of ancient Athenian democracy and the foundations of Western civilisation, yet its inner sanctums, which contained the cult statue of Athena, were inaccessible to all but a few priests. In many ways it acts reciprocally with the Agora, south of the Acropolis, which was not a physical thing, but a space for Athenians to assemble, and central to public, political, spiritual and commercial life. While the Parthenon symbolised freedom through culture and civilisation, the Agora was where it played out.

For much of architectural history, the question of style was a given: there was only one way to build. In the 19th century, however, styles began competing for the historical or moral value they were perceived or made to hold. For many Gothic Revivalists the style was a cipher for the religious practices and social structures of the Middle Ages, which stood in stark contrast to the upheavals wrought by the Industrial Revolution. For the designer and social reformer William Morris, style and morality were inseparable. He argued that the designer needed to become a craftsman once more, as a way of counteracting what he saw as the damaging effects of the division of labour and of industrialised production. For him, medieval styles were the natural reflection of this position, harking back to a time when designer and craftsman were one and the same. Thus, aesthetics became allied to social reform, at the root the idea that a particular style could in some way increase the freedom of its makers and users.

Although they differed in considerable and obvious ways, the idea that architecture had the potential for driving positive social change, as proposed by Morris and other Arts and Crafts thinkers, helped paved the way for Modernist architects' aspirations for an architecture that would reflect the new conditions of modernity. For Le Corbusier, modern architecture had the capability of mitigating the social 'unrest' that modernity had brought on. If society did not embrace modern architecture, he argued, then revolution would ensue: 'It is the question of building which lies at the root of the social unrest of today: architecture or revolution.'[3] In early Soviet Russia, before the turn to Socialist Realism and historicist styles, however, architecture and revolution were one and the same: architecture became an active instrument in trying to realise the new communist social order, with architects inventing new typologies to act as 'social condensers'. While Le Corbusier, in contrast, saw

Iktinos and Callicrates,
The Parthenon,
Athens,
447–432 BC

Replacing an earlier building, which can be pieced together from fragments held in the nearby Acropolis Museum, the Parthenon proclaimed Athens's pre-eminence as the cultural centre of the Ancient Greek world. The building itself is a perfectly proportioned peripteral octastyle Doric temple, adorned with sculptures of a then unprecedented naturalism and vigour. With the whole scheme overseen by the great sculptor Phidias, the Parthenon stands as the perfect union of sculpture and architecture – the cultural emblem of Athenian democracy and the foundations of Western civilisation.

Ancient Agora,
Athens,
6th century BC

Situated to the northwest of the Acropolis, the Agora was a kind of prototypical public space containing various temples and municipal buildings, as befitting its role as the social, cultural and political centre of the ancient city. The built structures were arranged around a central open area where citizens would gather, and which also functioned as a marketplace. Even when Athens's political and military power declined, the city remained an important cultural centre with the Agora at its epicentre.

DH Burnham & Co,
Flatiron Building,
175 Fifth Avenue,
New York City,
1902

The Flatiron Building is one of New York's most recognisable landmarks. Standing 20 storeys tall, the building's distinctive shape is the direct result of the triangular site created by the intersection of Fifth Avenue and East 22nd Street as they are cut across diagonally by Broadway. The Flatiron is the classic example of how Manhattan's gridded layout, which viewed on a plan in two dimensions might be expected to constrain architectural variety, actually yields a far more thrilling cityscape than if development had been allowed to proceed without a city plan.

Modernist architecture as a way of avoiding political revolution, whether in his Plan Voisin for Paris (1925) or Ville Radieuse (1930), he was similarly convinced that Modernist architecture and city planning could address the social ills of modernity, and transform every aspect of people's lives as powerfully as industrialisation had transformed the means of production.

Before the Second World War, Modernism's transformative spirit overrode any affiliation to a specific political ideology. It was variously taken on by both socialists and fascists – and many in between – and used in different guises as an instrument to further the freedom of individuals or collectives depending on the political context. However, after 1945, as Europe looked to chart its emergence from the ruins of the war, the transformations heralded by Modernism were taken on by social-democratic politicians who saw the opportunity to rebuild anew. New schools, hospitals, public buildings, not to mention countless housing estates, and even whole new towns rose from the destruction. During the postwar decades, most architects were employed by the public sector as the state took an unprecedentedly active role in all areas of society and economy. This was an era of righteous certainties and absolutes, admirable even if the realities of what was built did not always match the bold aspirations of its creators. Looking back at the worst excesses of postwar town planning and the most technocratically conceived housing estates, it is tempting to view the attempts at furthering the freedom of the collective as going too far and compromising individual freedoms.

Crisis Conditions

Today, after the so-called 'Neoliberal Revolution' of the 1980s, forever associated with Reagan and Thatcher, during which time a wave of privatisation and free market policies swept away the planned and tightly regulated economies of the postwar era, the pendulum has swung back the other way, towards the freedom of the individual. And after the global banking crisis of 2008, for many it has swung back too far. The change in the political-economic climate has affected every aspect of society, but its effects have been felt by the architectural profession particularly acutely. In the 1970s, most architects worked in the public sector, and most were involved in building (social) housing. Today, a tiny fraction of architects remain employed in the public sector, while almost all housing is built by and for the private sector, with many developments having little if any architect involvement.[4] More broadly, for decades architects have seen their traditional role diminish in scope as their responsibilities have been taken over by other disciplines within the construction industry. As a Royal Institute of British Architects (RIBA) report issued in the aftermath of the 2017 Grenfell Tower fire tragedy in London acknowledges: 'Developments in building procurement approaches mean that the Lead Designer (architect or engineer) is no longer responsible for oversight of the design and the specification of materials and products from inception to completion of the project, with design responsibility often transferred to the contractor and subcontractors, and no single point of responsibility.'[5]

Aesthetics became allied to social reform, at the root the idea that a particular style could in some way increase the freedom of its makers and users

Alison and Peter Smithson, Robin Hood Gardens, Poplar, London, 1972

Although among the most influential thinkers of their generation, Alison and Peter Smithson had to wait until the 1970s to put their ideas for housing into practice. At Robin Hood Gardens, the couple dealt with the difficult site by creating two blocks, with flats accessed by 'streets in the sky'. The blocks were arranged pincer-like around a central garden mound created from rubble from the slums that made way for the new development. Although revered by architects, the estate is widely viewed as a failure, and despite persistent campaigns to save it, demolition began in 2017.

PUP Architects,
Antepavilion,
Hoxton,
London,
2017

The Antepavilion is the first project in an annual initiative run by London's Architecture Foundation with sponsorship by the developer, Shiva, to create experimental rooftop structures in urban settings. Sited on the roof of Columbia Studios along the Regent's Canal, it takes the form of a two-storey air vent after the architects realised that this would be allowed by planning regulations. Functioning as a prototype micro-dwelling or summerhouse, the project acts as a poetic counterpoint to the sometimes stifling effects of planning.

Once upon a time, we might have seen architects as the conductor of the orchestra; now they are but one cog in a vast and increasingly complex machine.

Faced with this situation, many architects now feel that their profession is experiencing a crisis of agency. No longer, one could reasonably argue, do architects possess the ability to balance the demands of individual and collective freedoms that had previously defined their practice. This question provided the basis for a series of lectures and debates at the Royal Academy of Arts in London held in Autumn 2015, from which this issue of Δ has emerged.

Since then, in an attempt to find a way out of this crisis, the debate about how architects might reassert the importance of their role and influence has continued to grow louder. This came to the fore, for example, at Alejandro Aravena's Venice Architecture Biennale in 2016, which, as its title 'Reporting from the Front' suggested, argued for architects' unique role in 'taking care of the common good ... [and] expanding the frontiers of civilization'.[6] According to this view, it is imperative that architects reacquaint themselves with what many still believe to be the discipline's core mission of advancing social progress and promoting the public good, and at the same time expand the scope of their traditional disciplinary remit. While the intentions of those promoting such a way forward are often admirable, beyond the dilution of technical expertise, the risk here is that the example of the few socially engaged practices serve to legitimise the activities of the whole profession, some of which will inevitably be more ethically dubious.

The counterargument is that architects must refocus their attention on the internal demands of the discipline and the unique possibilities it can offer society, rather than wading into external debates and issues.[7] Yet architects cannot be immune to the changing contexts in which architecture exists – social and political, and, increasingly, digital. Walking into a room and realising that most people are not engaged with the space they are in, but with what is happening through their personal five-inch window into the online world, is now a familiar occurrence with a potentially transformative effect on how we think about and create architecture.

IF_DO,
After Image,
Dulwich Picture
Gallery,
London,
2017

Commissioned to celebrate the 200th anniversary of the opening of the Dulwich Picture Gallery in South London, the 'Dulwich Pavilion' was conceived by its designers to respond to the monumentality of Sir John Soane's adjacent gallery – a seminal building in the history of gallery design – and the comparative transience of its garden site. Over the summer of 2017, the building acted as a platform for events and activities organised by the gallery, and received significant press attention, raising the profile of its architects, a young, London-based practice.

Founded in memory of the late Richard Feilden, partner at UK architecture firm Feilden Clegg Bradley Studios, the Richard Feilden Foundation works to support and help improve the educational infrastructure available to children and young people in Africa with the hope that their projects will act as a model for other practices to follow. Working alongside engineers from BuroHappold, this project has included the creation of an open dining hall structure, new kitchen and latrines, classrooms and boarding accommodation.

It is tempting to view the attempts at furthering the freedom of the collective as going too far and compromising individual freedoms.

Architecture 00 was commissioned by the Ethical Property Company to turn a former shoe-polish factory in South London into a building that could accommodate various charitable organisations, as well as amenities such as a cafe and meeting rooms that were available for the use of the local community. The architects chose to retain much of the building, to which they added a new concrete-framed structure, with angled glazing and a rooftop pavilion with three gable ends echoing those of the original.

Finding Agency

Underlying both of these arguments is the question of freedom – for architects, and for the users and inhabitants of what they create. Can architects find the agency to reassert the balance between individual and collective freedom that is so fundamental to their practice, in the political-economic environment in which they currently operate? Or is it necessary to wait for those external conditions to change, or indeed even find ways to help facilitate those changes themselves? This issue of Ð tackles those questions head on. Through a variety of views and perspectives, it takes us to the heart of what freedom means for architecture in the 21st century.

The issue is split into three sections. The first focuses on identifying the limits that define the practice of architecture – the ones inherent to the discipline, and those deriving from personal or collective decisions and trends – through three distinct yet complementary essays. Peggy Deamer (pp 16–23) argues that architects cannot address the notion of freedom if their profession remains 'unfree', in its reliance on unpaid labour, and its lack of sexual and racial equality, among other examples. For South African architect Jo Noero (pp 24–31), whose work has long since engaged with the legacies of apartheid, every architectural decision has an ethical consideration that must be worked through, with the consequent paradox that the greatest freedom for the end user arguably occurs when the architect is most constrained. Ines Weizman explores this paradox within the context of 1970s Soviet Russia and the work of the 'paper architects', and also in our present moment where she argues the possibilities of preservation, documentation and copying can be used to inform different futures (pp 32–9).

The second section, on finding freedom, offers several case studies around architects' ability to shape the constraints of their practice, or find spaces where their impact can be lessened. The latter acts as the starting point for Sarah Wigglesworth in her exploration of the potential for self-initiated projects to allow architects to better define the parameters and ambitions of their work (pp 40–47). Alex Scott-Whitby, Anupama Kundoo and Kata Fodor (pp 48–53, 54–61 and 62–7) each explore their own personal and professional journeys to shape their practices at various stages of their careers and within different contexts. The question of what fundamentally distinguishes these journeys from other disciplines is taken on by Adam Nathaniel Furman in his argument that aesthetics ultimately define the practice of architecture, converting social relations and internal states into visual ones (pp 68–75). For him, architectural liberation lies in stylistic variety and aesthetic fecundity.

The third section considers architecture's capacity, as a physical and psychological construct, for making freedom, both for its users and for society. At one end of the spectrum, Patrik Schumacher makes a case for a libertarian form of freedom – for both society and architecture – which he argues can be achieved through parametricism and a 'soft architectural order' free of barriers and separation that allows for new forms of simultaneous social interaction (pp 76–83). From the other side, Anna Minton (pp 84–91) considers how mass privatisation has played out since the 1970s, and argues that the resulting urban securitisation poses a considerable threat to freedom and democracy. Somewhere in the middle, Carlo Cappai and Maria Alessandra Segantini of C+S Architects consider the possibility of hybridised spaces (pp 92–101), which in the case of their numerous school projects fulfil their primary function and also act as spatial resources for communities

Arthur Mamou-Mani,
Polibot: The DNA of Making,
Arup headquarters,
London,
October 2017

Architect Arthur Mamou-Mani argues that robotic technologies will be central to the future of construction, heralding a revolution not just in how we create buildings, but also how we see and understand them. Unlike existing construction robotics that are based on the robotic arms used in the car industry, Mamou-Mani's Polibot is a cable construction robot, able to both build and then take down buildings. In this way, it shows how future demolition can be anticipated and therefore facilitated in the design and construction of buildings, reflecting a new circular economy.

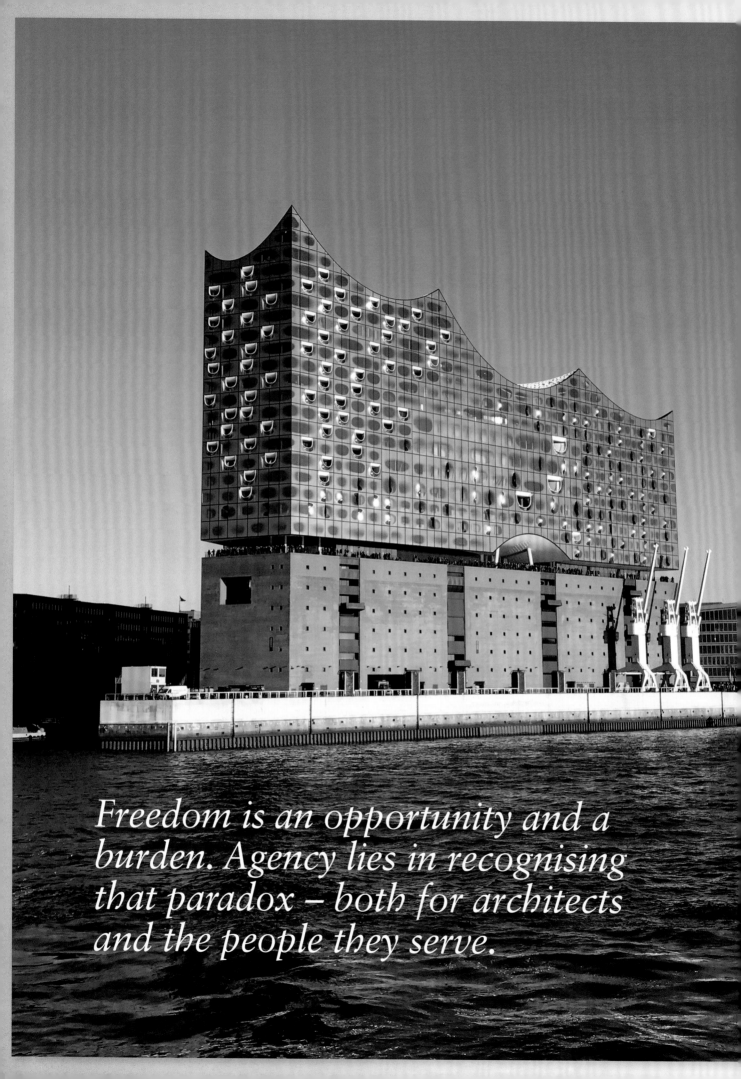

Freedom is an opportunity and a burden. Agency lies in recognising that paradox – both for architects and the people they serve.

to develop new social and economic relations. Stepping aside from arguments regarding diminishing agency and power, Charles Holland (pp 102–9) explores a 'counter narrative' visible in a range of self-build and cooperative projects where architects work more as enablers and facilitators of 'bottom-up' initiatives, effecting small but meaningful change that opens the door to greater strategic influence. This is followed by interviews with two practitioners, Kate Goodwin and Usman Haque (pp 110–19 and 120–27), who from a traditional viewpoint might be seen as operating on the margins of the profession, but whose work, respectively, in curating and creative programming, and using technological tools to empower people in cities, points to issues critical to architecture's future.

Although the articles in the issue diverge considerably in subject, focus, and professional and political viewpoint, uniting them all is the consistent idea that freedom is not an absolute or even an ideal, but a paradox. For architects, indeed for society itself, freedom can be both limiting and enabling – and the constraints we feel can be likewise. The essays make clear that freedom and agency are vital for architects, yet they also illustrate the extent to which constraints – practical, political and philosophical – are fundamental to their practice. Just as a tight brief or tricky site can paradoxically enable the best work, so the discipline itself needs those constraints to exist – and it is often when they are tightest that new ideas and new directions emerge. Rand's notion of architecture as a search for total freedom was misguided, not because that quest was impossible (although it was), but because the premise of the question was wrong. Freedom is an opportunity and a burden. Agency lies in recognising that paradox – both for architects and the people they serve. ⌂

Notes
1. Ayn Rand, *The Fountainhead*, Granada (St Albans), 1983, p 134.
2. See Kirstin Powers, 'Donald Trump's "Kinder, Gentler" Version', *USA Today*, 11 April 2016: www.usatoday.com/story/opinion/2016/04/11/donald-trump-interview-elections-2016-ayn-rand-vp-pick-politics-column/82899566/.
3. Le Corbusier, *Towards a New Architecture*, trans Frederick Etchells, Butterworth Architecture (London), 1989, p 269, quoted by Neil Leach in 'Architecture or Revolution?', *Architecture and Revolution: Contemporary Perspectives on Central and Eastern Europe*, Routledge (London and New York), 1999, p 122.
4. For example, in the UK: 'In the 1970s 50% of architects were employed by the public sector, now less than 9% are.' RIBA, *The Future for Architects?*, RIBA Building Futures report, 2011: www.buildingfutures.org.uk/assets/downloads/The_Future_for_Architects_Full_Report_2.pdf.
5. 'RIBA Statement on Design for Fire Safety', 22 June 2017: www.architecture.com/knowledge-and-resources/knowledge-landing-page/riba-statement-on-design-for-fire-safety.
6. Alejandro Aravena, 'Curatorial Proposal' for the Venice Architecture Biennale, 2016: www.labiennale.org/en/architecture/2016/intervento-di-alejandro-aravena.
7. Patrik Schumacher, 'Where is the Architecture? – Appraisal of the Venice Architecture Biennale 2016': www.patrikschumacher.com/Texts/Where%20is%20Architecture_Appraisal%20of%20the%20Venice%20Architecture%20Biennale%202016.html. Also published in *Icon*, 158, August 2016.

Herzog & de Meuron,
Elbphilharmonie,
Hamburg,
2016

Making startling use of a redundant 1960s warehouse building, the Elbphilharmonie combines a hotel with concert venues and a dramatic publicly accessible viewing platform between the brick warehouse and the glass superstructure. Taking nearly 10 years to complete, the project was subject to repeated delays and concerted political pressures, but emerged as one of the most scintillating and dramatic buildings of recent years – iconic without being an exercise in arbitrary form-making.

David Isaac Hecht,
Becca at Work,
The Multidisciples,
Columbia Graduate School of Architecture,
Planning and Preservation (GSAPP),
New York,
2015

David Hecht: 'Architecture school produces professional knowledge workers who regulate themselves into performance at the extremes of productivity, mental and physical health, and susceptibility to exploitation. The Multidisciples project suggests that, in order to render that process visible, we might look at how the bodies of students are configured and ultimately inscribed into the apparatus of a complex of discipline, control and subjectivation in the service of a capitalist machine.'

Peggy Deamer

(Un)Free Work

Architecture, Labour and Self-Determination

Does the very nature of architectural practice preclude architects from creating spaces that foster freedom for their users? And what is freedom anyway? **Peggy Deamer** – a practising architect and Professor of Architecture at Yale University – sets out her point of view. Citing theorists from Karl Marx to Theodor Adorno and from Michel Foucault to Slavoj Zizek, she examines the particular challenges presented to architects by Neoliberalism, and discusses how they might generate a healthier working and living climate for all.

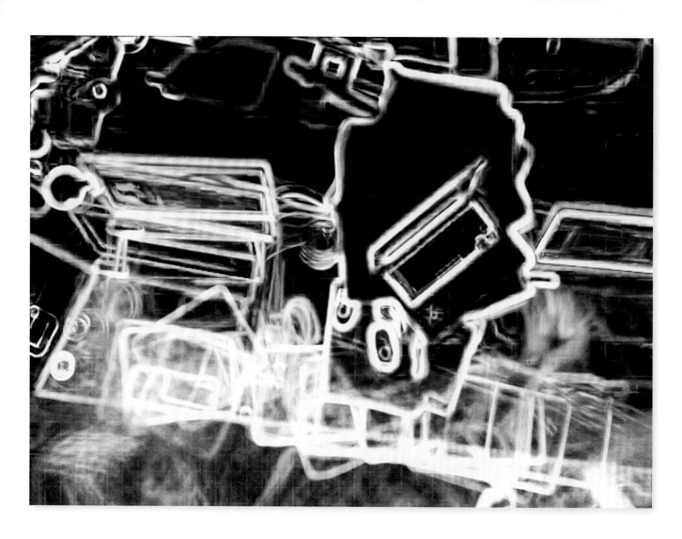

Clearly the production of freedom may not be the immediate programme of the majority of our architectural work, but our liberal education, our code of ethics, and our roots in humanism make it the horizon of our disciplinary conscience.

David Isaac Hecht,
Cici at Work,
The Multidisciples,
Columbia GSAPP,
New York,
2015

David Hecht: 'The images present observations of the working conditions of students in various studio setups during the spring semester of 2015. A technique inspired by the time-motion studies of Frank and Lillian Gilbreth was developed to investigate relationships between the body of the student (considered as a worker) and the arrangement of the workspace (both on an individual level, and as constrained by the institution).'

Ben at Work,
The Multidisciples,
2015

'The method for producing the images involved the fabrication of a specialised camera rig, implementation of stop-motion capture software on a camera phone, and integration and custom processing in Adobe Photoshop and After Effects. Videos and still images were then generated to provide multiple objects for consideration.'

The premise is a simple one: architecture cannot produce spaces of freedom – public spaces, healthy spaces, accessible spaces, affordable spaces, sensually liberating spaces – for the society architects presume to serve if they are produced in unfree circumstances such as unpaid labour, gender inequality, generational hegemony, unsustainable work hours, non-existent work–life balance, lack of collegiality or discipline-crippling competition. This is not primarily an argument for the link between production and product, however, which would suggest that all that is being said is that there is a connection between the mode of labour and the 'use' or 'exchange' value of the product. There certainly is such a connection: Karl Marx has made the point that 'concrete labour' (labour that is subjectively offered) is associated with use value while 'abstract labour' (that which is divided and quantified) is associated with exchange value. According to Marx, the ability to abstract and quantify human labour (labour power) is linked to the historical development of economic exchange in general, and commodity trade (the trade in wares and merchandise) more specifically.[1] In the 19th century, John Ruskin made the point in *The Seven Lamps of Architecture* (1849) that an immoral society that did not appreciate the need for labourers to be creative and self-empowered could not produce 'moral' buildings.[2] In the 20th century Theodor Adorno, the German philosopher and leading member of the Frankfurt School, claimed that functionalism in architecture – by which he meant not its practicality, but its sensuous meaning – cannot exist in an irrational society.[3] And Manfredo Tafuri, the Italian architecture theorist, insisted that a capitalist society could not generate architecture that does not serve capitalist aims.[4] The relationship between how things are produced and the true value of what is produced is therefore not worth contesting; at some level, it is obvious.

Barriers to Freedom
The premise being presented here, however, is more nuanced than this, addressing the ability of a producing subject (the architect) to grasp the product (freedom) that is presumably the object(ive) of his or her labour. This itself implies two things: firstly, that it is not a question of whether the architect is capable of producing freedom, but rather whether he or she is able to identify it as a concept; and secondly, that the concern is also not primarily about the external circumstances that hinder the production of freedom, but the personal, subjective circumstances that inhibit its initial imago. Certainly there are external factors outside architects' control that limit the possibility of producing 'free' spaces: private clients whose ambitions are anything but publicly oriented; government-issued zoning laws serving money-making development; a litigious society determining contractual relationships shaped around risk mitigation versus generosity and opportunity; standards of construction that privilege the hegemonic status quo; trade relationships that distribute and privilege certain goods unfairly; antitrust laws that prevent disciplinary cooperation. In short, capitalism offers innumerable barriers to both free production and free products. But again, what is being posed here is the ability of architects to conceive of freedom such that they can even initiate the task of producing it and battling the external hindrances.

Clearly the production of freedom may not be the immediate programme of the majority of our architectural work, but our liberal education, our code of ethics, and our roots in humanism make it the horizon of our disciplinary conscience. But what is freedom? Access to choice? The end of alienation? Autonomy?

Self-determination? All are debatable and all have ideological underpinnings that make not just their possibility fraught, but their allure deceptive. Slavoj Zizek, the Slovenian continental philosopher, has pointed out that we actually do not want to be free; that freedom is anxiety producing and in our heart-of-hearts we seek the safety of limited options.[5] Critics of American Neoliberalism, including psychologists, suggest that in a country that now values autonomy above all else, freedom can become a type of tyranny imposed by an ideology of economics and rational choice, a mindset that leads to perpetual dissatisfaction with our lives.[6] Nevertheless, subjective self-determination – even incomplete or compromised – is a sine qua non for pondering the difficult path of personal, social and cultural freedom. As the French philosopher Michel Foucault has said: 'There are times in life when the question of knowing whether one can think differently than one thinks, and perceive differently than one sees, is absolutely necessary if one is to go on looking and reflecting at all.'[7] For us architects, freedom (or self-determination) is illusive not because it is ambiguous, contradictory or uncontested, but because it is an abstraction. In other words, it is not that we cannot agree on a definition of freedom or that we cannot trust in its possibility; rather, as long as it is not experienced, it is unknowable.

David Isaac Hecht,
Leah at Work,
The Multidisciples,
Columbia GSAPP,
New York,
2015

David Hecht: 'Recordings were made at different times over the course of a week near the end of the semester. Each captures around one hour of mostly digital work by MArch students in different years of the graduate programme. Most of the images were processed so as to expose visually variation in body position relative to technical equipment and workspace over time, but in a mode that is neither easily quantified nor simply interpreted through normal techniques of visual inspection.'

Architecture can be exposed for what it is: a profession providing the 'unfree' working conditions ... that have long since been mitigated in other disciplines.

David Isaac Hecht,
Mitch at Work,
The Multidisciples,
Columbia GSAPP,
New York,
2015

'The process stands in contrast to the Gilbreth studies, which were a development on Taylorist practices, and sought to produce quantitatively analysable objects through the ocular capture of movement over time, for the purposes of optimising productivity through organising and disciplining workers' bodies and technical equipment.'

Abstraction

The role of abstraction in obfuscating the true meaning of a term is indicated by Marx's distinction between abstract and concrete labour, where, as indicated above, it is associated with the transformation of experienced labour into its market value. Marx argues that the abstraction of labour is part of a process in which commercial trade in products not only alters the way labour is viewed, but also how it is practically treated. In other words, when labour becomes a commercial object traded in the marketplace, then the form and content of work in the workplace will be transformed as well. Abstraction and commodification go hand in hand. But the critique of abstract thought goes beyond Marx and labour. The Frankfurt School, the early 20th-century Neo-Marxist German think tank, described the pride of 'reason' that tears the individual away from a life of genuine wants and needs.[8] Abstraction, associated with rationality, was implicated for its distancing of the subject from felt life and allowing totalitarianism to appear acceptable. Further, Michael Hardt and Antonio Negri's discourse on affect in *Empire*, their influential book on contemporary power in which emotional, sensual and caring life is designated as the realm of both value and exploitation,[9] and Foucault's on biopolitics, where the body becomes the locus for hegemonic colonisation, are linked in their study of 'lived' authority: biopower is understood to target affect as part of its controlling mechanism; at the same time, affective life may be an 'outside' that exceeds biopolitical mechanisms. Affect and biopolitics share a starting point: attending to affective life orients inquiry into how new ways of living may emerge.[10] As the contemporary Italian media theorist Matteo Paquinelli has suggested in addressing 'the essential problem (of) the politics of abstraction', capitalism continues to evolve towards ever more sophisticated and abstract algorithms that allow it to maintain its control over social networks, global logistics and financial transactions.[11] To combat this, as Baruch Spinoza in the 17th century, Rudolph Steiner in the late 19th century, and Gilles Deleuze in the 20th century have said, one must operate in the context of 'living work'.[12]

Architecture can be exposed for what it is: a profession providing the 'unfree' working conditions identified in the opening premise of this article that have long since been mitigated in other disciplines. It is precisely these working conditions that contrast with what we, as architects, have been trained to admire and produce: a humanitarian life. What is of interest, then, is how architects have not only failed to make the connection between our working conditions and our work, but actively deceived ourselves into believing that we are uniquely qualified to make judgements addressing social equitability and humanitarian spaces.

On the one hand, this can be explained by a uniquely architectural form of ideology. The discourses of creativity, collaboration and innovation that permeate Neoliberalism are particularly applicable to architecture; we congratulate ourselves for always having been what the rest of the knowledge economy is now extolling: a 'lab' culture that bypasses corporatism and office protocols. In this self-congratulation, we substitute the myth of creativity for the reality of our daily experience; capitalist ideology has convinced us that architecture serves a social purpose while hiding its actual real-estate-driven agenda.

On the other hand, we can see it as a more complex (and architecturally tilted) version of the schizophrenia that Deleuze and Félix Guattari have described as capitalism's natural consequence.[13] In architecture, this schizophrenic state is our polarised identity as creator versus worker. Despite the fact that we go to an office, get

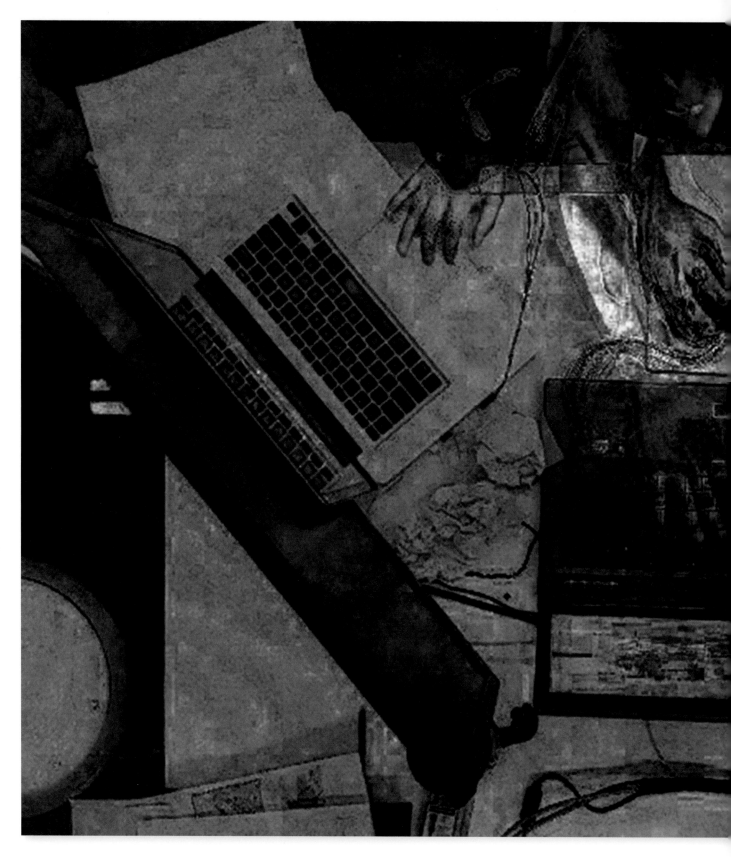

David Isaac Hecht,
Mustafa at Work,
The Multidisciples,
Columbia GSAPP,
New York,
2015

David Hecht: 'The images remain within a visual regime, but seek
to obscure possibilities for optimisation in favour of exposing the
process of subjectivisation enacted through modulation; that is, the
repetitive implementation of the (micro)techniques of disciplinary
power through the structural and informational regulation enacted
within the institution of the university.'

a pay cheque and fill out our time sheet, architects bypass these evident characteristics of 'work' and emphasise, instead, 'art'. This failure of identity has many secondary schizo- consequences – aristocratic/privileged versus middle class; management versus labour – but the overall effect is a total ignorance of labour discourse and, consequently, any grasp of the reality of our daily work life. We are dutifully shocked by the unjust treatment of nail-salon workers, fashion models or graduate teaching assistants while never making the connection to our own work circumstances.

Architecture, Affect and Freedom

We do not want to insist that the architectural profession can operate outside capitalist structure to affectively 'live' freedom and thereby produce it. That would be naive. However, one can resist the models of work – the division of labour, lack of creative autonomy of all workers, disappearance of work/life balance – that are the acceptable norm and become a template of a socially organised profession. The goal of an emancipated work environment would not be measured by absolute standards of freedom (impossible, as we have indicated), but by constant work on the contingency of our affective life. On the one hand this would be, in effect, the reversal of work that organises our bodies into productive design labour (not entirely different to how Fordist factory labour shaped us through a series of repeated, cyclical steps); and on the other it would measure success in terms other than profit or aesthetic kudos. It would not be an easy organisational fix, but a commitment to respect all individuals involved – staff, consultants, firm owners, managers, clients – as they articulate their visions and angsts, their strengths and weaknesses, their self-determined value. It means everyone becoming involved in solving problems and making decisions that affect all of our lives. The fact that architecture is connected to other disciplines that conform to Neoliberalism's competitive demands does not mean that in our own homes we cannot experiment with what freedoms we actually control. ↺

Notes
1. 'Introduction', *Grundrisse 01*, 1857: www.marxists.org/archive/marx/works/1857/grundrisse/ch01.htm#3.
2. John Ruskin, *The Seven Lamps of Architecture*, Dover Publications (New York) 1989.
3. Theodor Adorno, 'Functionalism Today', in Neil Leach (ed), *Rethinking Architecture: A Reader in Cultural Theory*, Routledge (London), 1997, pp 5–18.
4. Manfredo Tafuri, *Architecture and Utopia: Design and Capitalist Development*, trans Barbara Luigia La Penta, MIT Press (Cambridge, MA), 1999.
5. Slavoj Zizek, 'What is Freedom Today?', video: www.theguardian.com/commentisfree/video/2014/dec/03/slavoj-zizek-philosopher-what-is-freedom-today-video.
6. Barry Schwartz, 'Self-Determination: The Tyranny of Freedom', *American Psychologist*, 55 (1), January 2000, pp 79–88: www.swarthmore.edu/SocSci/bschwar1/self-determination.pdf.
7. Michel Foucault, 1978 talk quoted by Gilles Deleuze in Ben Anderson, 'Affect and Biopower: Towards a Politics of Life', *Transactions of the Institute of British Geographers*, 22 November 2010, pp 142–3: www.scribd.com/document/305612301/Affect-and-Biopower-Ben-Anderson.
8. Max Horkheimer and Theodor Adorno, *Dialectic of Enlightenment: Philosophical Fragments*, ed Gunzelin Schmid Noerr, trans Edmund Jephcott, Stanford University Press (Stanford, CA), 2002.
9. Michael Hardt and Antonio Negri, *Empire*, Harvard University Press (Cambridge, MA), 2000.
10. For the relationship between affect and biopower, see Anderson, *op cit*.
11. Matteo Pasquinelli, 'The Politics of Abstraction: Beyond the Opposition of Knowledge and Life', *Open!*, 14 October 2013: http://matteopasquinelli.com/politics-of-abstraction/.
12. Anderson, *op cit*.
13. Gilles Deleuze and Félix Guattari, *Anti-Oedipus: Capitalism and Schizophrenia*, trans Robert Hurley, University of Minnesota Press (Minneapolis, MN), 1983.

Jo Noero

Limits to Freedom

Liberating Form, Programme and Ethics

According to Cape Town-based architect **Jo Noero**, there is no reason why a complex brief should restrict architectural creativity and vision. But what are the keys to achieving the right balance between ethics, aesthetics, and fitness for initial and possible future purposes? Drawing on the writings of several theorists, he examines architecture's moral dimension and seeks out strategies for designing freely, ethically and effectively.

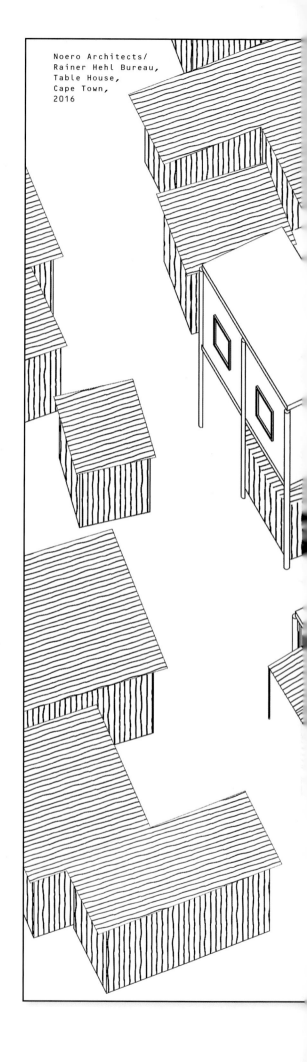

Noero Architects/
Rainer Hehl Bureau,
Table House,
Cape Town,
2016

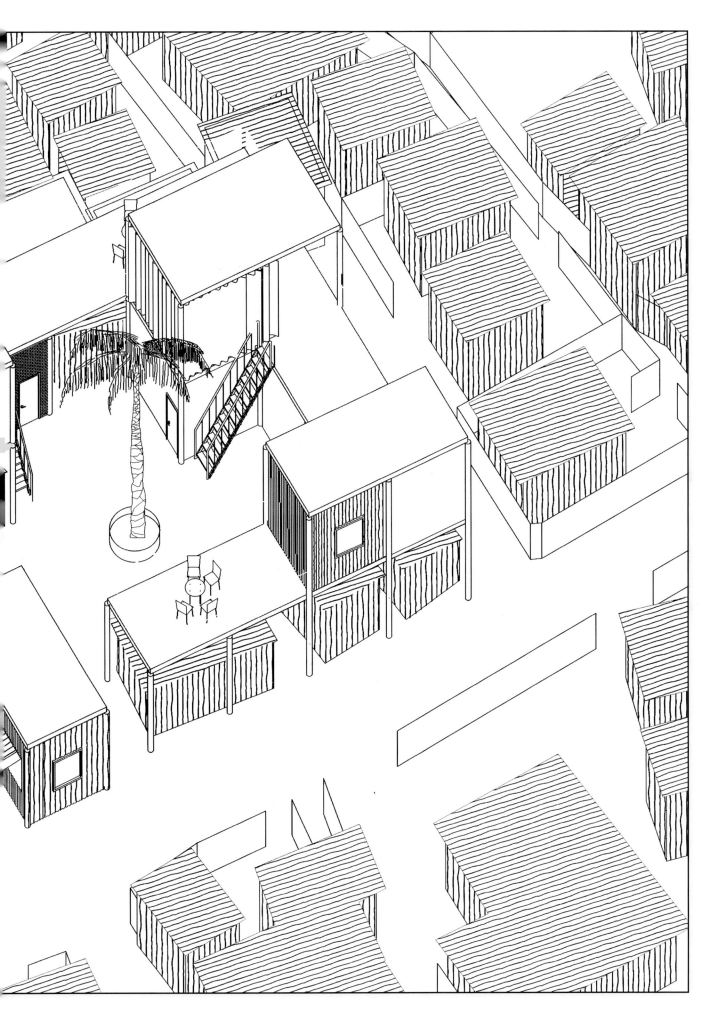

'I claim for myself the rights and liberties that painters and poets have held for so long.'
— Pancho Guedes[1]

This quote highlights the confusion that lies at the heart of what constitutes architecture in today's world. Architecture is not like a poetic or dramatic work; it is a practical art made to satisfy purpose. Without purpose, architecture cannot exist![2] Architects cannot be given the freedom to make architecture as they wish. To do so would fundamentally change architecture and would render it of no use to society. Equally there is nothing to be gained in arguing that revolution, which offers the idea of new kinds of freedom, is necessary to develop a socially useful and appropriate architecture. The sociological theorist Peter Berger wrote extensively on this subject: he demonstrated the fallacy of revolution in the 20th century and the sacrifices that were made for a mostly unrealised future gain.[3] Similarly architecture does not possess the power to change the world. At best it can help matters along; at worst it can be hideous.

Critics argue that architecture is in crisis. The architectural theorist and critic Neil Leach has written that architects have retreated into the boudoir – an arcane world of abstract spatial art.[4] Autonomous form has stripped architecture of all meaning other than as novel form. At the heart of this lies the silly idea that architects need freedom from all kinds of social constraints to make form: this is poisonous and has reduced the value of architecture to that of the image only.

How can architecture recover its value to society as a practical, social, cultural and aesthetic art? To start off, one could consider the idea that architecture is a purposeful practical art which carries within it an important ethical dimension.

The clue to understanding this is provided by the 20th-century philosopher Ludwig Wittgenstein, who wrote that ethics is 'the enquiry into what is valuable' or into 'what is really important', 'the meaning of life', 'what makes life worth living' or 'the right way of living'.[5] When the purpose for which the work of architecture is intended satisfies this definition, one can say that the architect has acted ethically.

The following ideas offer ways of thinking about architecture so that people can be exposed to new readings of space and in turn could be free to use buildings in previously unimagined ways.

Form can symbolise freedom, but it does not necessarily lead to freedom. Human agency is both fickle and unpredictable – what is built to represent freedom can, in a revolutionary moment, be transformed into something very different. The National Stadium of Chile, built in Santiago in 1938, was used to celebrate the election of the Socialist government led by Salvador Allende in 1971 and was an important cultural, sporting and political symbol of the new regime. After the coup by Augusto Pinochet and the CIA in 1973, in which Allende was deposed, the changing rooms in the stadium were used as interrogation and torture chambers and the grass of the playing field was soaked with the blood of people who had been executed.

Architects do not posses the freedom of the fine artist, poet or sculptor when they make work. It is useful to consider the differences that exist between architecture and the other arts, given that architecture is viewed as an art, albeit a practical one. These differences – purpose, publicness, site, technology and structure – show that the freedom offered to the architect is more circumscribed than what is enjoyed by fine artists. Richard Serra, the noted US

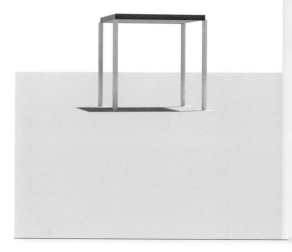

Noero Architects/
Rainer Hehl Bureau,
Table House,
Cape Town,
2016

The prototype under construction. The work illustrated took two days to complete and was built by Hands of Honor, a social business involved in reusing throwaway products. The people involved in the construction process had never built anything before.

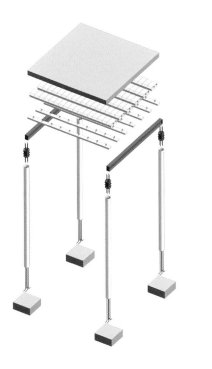

The basic conception of the Table House (left) refers to the 'primitive hut', as propounded by the 18th-century theorist Marc-Antoine Laugier. However, as shown by the assembly diagram (right), even when working at the lowest possible cost, architects are still required to exercise their skills to the fullest extent imaginable.

Two ways of imagining how to use the Table House over time. The first (left) consists of individual households building vertically, thus liberating open green space. The second (right) demonstrates the possibility of using the Table House to construct social housing in which walls are common and circulation is shared.

sculptor, studied at Yale University in the 1960s when fine arts and architecture shared common studio spaces. He was asked, given the spatial focus in his work, why he did not become an architect. His answer was very clear: he said he was a sculptor because, as an architect, he would have had to make purposeful space in which he had no interest.[6]

If architecture is a practical art and the satisfaction of purpose implies an ethical dimension, it follows that the architect should take into consideration all the people who are affected by the work. This inclusive approach can lead to new understandings of space and its use. Paradoxically the more dense and inclusive the programme – in other words the less freedom offered to the architect in terms of the brief – the greater the potential for opening up the architecture and its spaces to new understandings and uses. In turn this gives greater freedom to the people who use the spaces. The Table House project in Cape Town, designed by Noero Architects and Rainer Hehl Bureau, illustrates this idea. After many months of negotiation and discussion, the idea of the Table House emerged as a prototype for incremental housing. The process involved both an expansion of programme to include a great variety of potential elements, and an opposite but equal reduction of the architecture which in its final form is minimal. The first prototype was built in 2016 in Cape Town. The Table House, as an archetype, represents freedom since it can act as a stimulus to encourage people to imagine a variety of different ways to both make and use the spaces of their homes.

Architecture cannot be reduced to the slogan of 'form follows function' or 'form follows purpose'. Purpose and form need to interact with each other iteratively in the design process until a satisfactory set of spaces and structures is achieved. This process is both rational and intuitive, and the outcome depends on the skill and talent of the architect. It can be said that the best work is made when the architect produces a building whose purpose has led to an imaginative and poetic outcome. It is at this moment that the possibility of offering freedom in whatever form to the users is achieved.

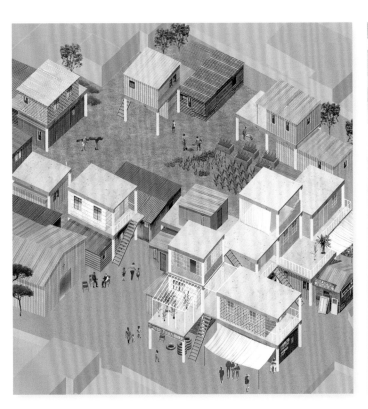

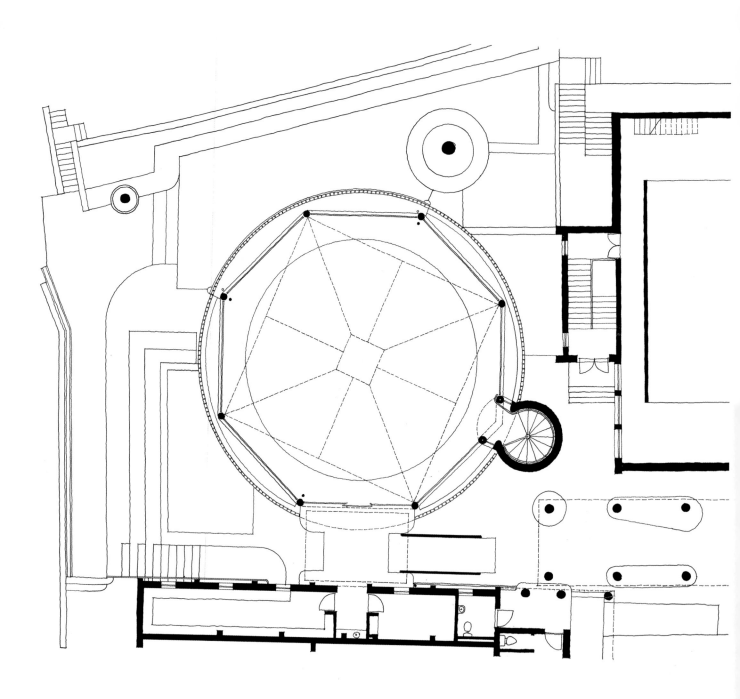

Architects should embrace
the programme in all its
complexities, to develop denser
readings of what architecture
could become.

Noero Architects,
Life Centre,
St Cyprian's Girls School,
Cape Town,
2012

Plan. The building was designed to
be as flexible as possible, since its
intended purpose was in the process
of being changed by the Curriculum
Committee of the Ministry of National
Education.

Interior view. The forms marry
geometric precision with
freedom of use.

Programme and Ethics

Freedom implies certain ethical and moral imperatives, since it
would have no meaning without them. If this is so, where precisely
does one locate ethics in the work of the architect? As discussed
above, purpose, programme and use are elements that should
lead to ethical outcomes. In turn, this set of ideas can be traced
to the transactional relationship that exists between architect and
client. In this regard the programme is fundamentally important
since the architect is called upon to act on it to give shape to the
architecture. It is at this moment that the architect is required to
make an ethical judgment: what is the purpose of the building,
who are the clients and whom should the architect address in
determining the programme? This is essential to ensure that the
appropriate values and issues are canvassed to give the project
form. More often than not, the programme is seen by the architect
as an obstacle to creativity, and in many cases is simplified to make
life easier for both architect and client. This is wrong. Architects
should embrace the programme in all its complexities, to develop
denser readings of what architecture could become. In turn this
could lead to an architecture of greater freedom because of the
heightened possibilities of use offered up by the spaces. There is also
the question of the conflict which can arise between the needs of the
client and of those who use the building. In this regard, the public
good is of paramount importance: if in the process of designing a
building's spaces the public good is compromised in any significant
way, the architect is obliged to act; failure to do so would mean that
the architect is ethically compromised.

Noero Architects,
Christ Church,
Somerset West,
Cape Town,
under construction

Plan and sectional perspective.
The plan form comprises
a circle within a truncated
square. The section shows
two spaces – one vertical
and the other horizontal. This
allows for varying numbers of
congregants from 50 to 900
people. Construction began
in 2016.

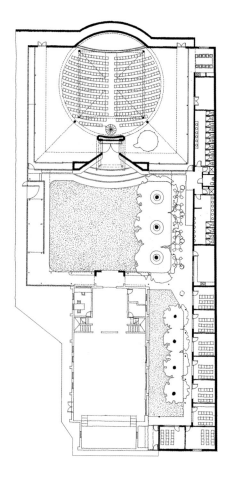

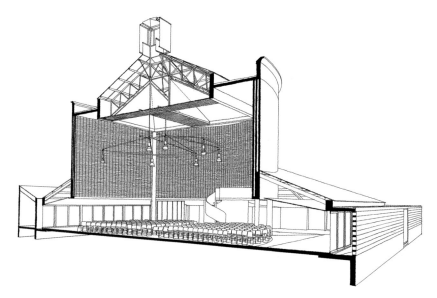

Interior view. The circular
central area gives precise
meaning as a religious space,
while together with the
lower flanking areas it can
be used also for more
everyday functions.

Noero Architects,
St Paul's Anglican Church,
Jabavu,
White City,
Soweto,
Johannesburg,
1984

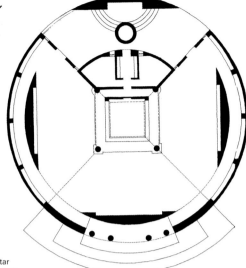

Plan and cutaway
perspective. The altar
space is placed centrally
and the quadrant behind
this space is given to an
external altar. The inside
space can be used by
groups from 50 to 500
people by employing the
quadrants in different
ways.

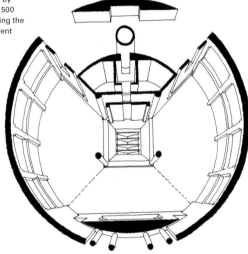

The external altar faces onto
a large courtyard that can
accommodate 4,000 people.

Spatial and Formal Strategies

Assuming that the architect has made an ethically appropriate decision regarding programme, the strategy that he or she chooses to determine form can be difficult. Agency has the capacity to change use, which can render the original programme and form indifferent or even redundant. What spatial and formal strategies are open to ensure that the original programme for the building is appropriate and resolved and yet is still open to new uses over time? It could be said that satisfying this set of conditions would get close to achieving an architecture of freedom. Aldo Rossi, the Italian architect and theorist, offers up the most compelling argument in this regard. As a result of the research he had undertaken on city form, public buildings and monuments, in his book *Architecture of the City* he speculated that those buildings marked by a precise geometry were best able to adjust to changing uses over time.[7]

Three examples from the work of Noero Architects are shown here which build on this idea of Rossi's. The first is the Life Centre, a building at St Cyprian's Girls School in Cape Town, designed to accommodate many different purposes – from drama, to indoor hockey, to music, to yoga. Completed in 2012, this has a plan form which is geometrically precise and has been able to accommodate both original needs as well as new ones that have emerged since the building was finished. The second and third projects consist of two churches: St Paul's Church in Jabavu, White City, Soweto, completed in 1985, and Christ Church in Cape Town, currently under construction. Both of these churches were made to accommodate religious services large and small as well as many other uses such as theatre, community meeting spaces, banquets and weddings. The challenge was to create spaces that would have a spiritual quality but which could also open up to more prosaic functions.

The work that architects make reflects their values and is, in this sense, autobiographical. However, at the same time the work is made on behalf of others, and the programme and aspirations of the commissioning body need to be satisfied. This tension is only healthy when the autobiographical expression of the architect is held in careful check by an ethical sensibility. Rather than give architects freedom to make space in whatever way they imagine, what is needed is an architecture which in its programme, order, spaces and uses offers up freedom to the people who use it. ᴆ

Notes
1. Pancho Guedes, *Manifestos, Papers, Lectures and Publications*, Ordem dos Arquitectos (Lisbon), 2007, p 146.
2. Colin St John Wilson, *The Other Tradition of Modernity*, Academy Editions (London), 1995, p 46.
3. See, for example, Peter L Berger, *Movement and Revolution*, Anchor Press/Doubleday (New York), 1970, pp 14–27.
4. Neil Leach, *The Anaesthetics of Architecture*, MIT Press (Cambridge, MA and London), 1999, pp 18–33.
5. Ludwig Wittgenstein, 'A Lecture on Ethics' (1929), *Philosophical Review*, 74, January 1965, pp 2–12.
6. Richard Serra in conversation with the author at the home of Emily Pulitzer, St Louis, Missouri, September 1997.
7. Aldo Rossi, *The Architecture of the City*, MIT Press (Cambridge, MA), 1982, pp 28–57.

Experiments in Digital
Documentation of
Adolf Loos's Vienna Houses

ARCHITEC
INTERNAL

Ines Weizman

TURE'S EXILE

Barbora Tothova
and María Diego,
Photogrammetry
of a staircase,
Scheu House,
Vienna (1912/13),
'Stealing Spaces:
The Digital
Reconstruction
of Modernism',
Centre for
Documentary
Architecture,
Bauhaus-Universität
Weimar, Germany,
2017

In the Festschrift for Adolf Loos's 60th birthday, Mrs Scheu wrote that there is only one building in Vienna that is more beautiful than the house on Michaelerplatz: her house.

Digital documentation in architecture usually focuses entirely on form – but architectural professor **Ines Weizman** sees ways of using it more imaginatively. As Director of the Centre for Documentary Architecture at the Bauhaus-Universität Weimar, she recently led a research project investigating the domestic work of Adolf Loos in the 1910s–20s and how it has evolved since. Here she presents its background and results, which reveal not only the material evidence but the stories behind it.

Based at the Bauhaus-Universität Weimar, the Centre for Documentary Architecture (CDA) is an interdisciplinary project that explores buildings as documents and built environments as archives in which history is inscribed. Architects, filmmakers, artists and theorists undertake collective and individual research projects – ranging from publications, exhibitions and installations to films, new media projects and public programmes – in contested areas or historical periods where architecture could be used as a registrar of political relations and transformations. This article is part of a series of such interventions that trace the otherwise familiar history of modernism as a networked set of encounters between people and things in movement. Navigating the deep space of architectural history across physical and cultural borders, we can explore how personal, sometimes intimate histories have become entrapped in the aftermath of political ideologies: namely national socialism, colonialism, real-existing communism and neo-liberalism. The approach guiding this project began with a documentary project that aimed to digitally scan details, interiors and fragments of well-known houses designed by Adolf Loos in Vienna in the early 20th century. The close reading of architectural fragments that also involved digital documentation allowed the afterlives of those iconic sites of architecture to be retraced, and offered a striking world – a space of freedom, or escape perhaps – in which architecture could both be re-enacted but also expanded into a unique historical space.

Before presenting the documentary project, a few thoughts on the idea of freedom of movement and its interaction with architecture: Freedom is a fundamental human right. It is the power to believe, think, speak and act of one's own volition, without undue interference. While all creative gestures essentially rely upon this freedom, it is in its absence that, paradoxically, a new and delicate space of action and imagination may open up. In the same way as dissidents of the Soviet Bloc in the 1970s and 1980s created a world of 'inner migration', a place in which they found their own personal freedom, today, the potential sites of freedom extend to the ability to move across borders involving also digital environments, virtual realities, social media networks and new possibilities of leaking. In the same way as whistleblowers and leakers have transgressed borders, gender politics and social organising, architecture's internal exile might be articulated as an exodus from the tyranny of digital surveillance and architectural software designed for the purpose of replicating forms – still inhabiting technological space, but functioning as a more inventive domain of digital subversion.

Fantasy Versus Utopia

Moscow's so-called 'paper architects' offered fascinating documents in this regard. Employed in state-run architectural collectives, or as staff in architecture schools, architects and artists such as Iskander Galimov, Mikhail Belov, Alexander Brodsky and Ilya Utkin, Mikhail Filippov, Nadia Bronzova and Yuri Avvakumov were meeting in private houses – kitchens, as they later liked to tell – to produce the kind of drawings that meant to challenge the 'stifling' standardised language of Soviet architecture, and to introduce 'culture', understood largely as national and religious tradition, into architectural articulation of allegories, legends and postmodern contextualisation. Their drawings and etchings depicted outlandish, often impossible, structures and cityscapes displaying a high level of intricacy and great efforts applied in their creation.

The antiquated and operose gesture of the needle cutting into the plate and the romanticism and melancholia of their motives exhibit a sense of despair that in its sheer 'inefficiency', absurd lethargy and bizarre search for beauty could be understood as a political statement.[1] The escape into an 'internal world' presented a form of refusal to accept the functionalist environment of socialism. As such, dissent was articulated by stylistic irony, by the use of pencil and watercolours, rather than the modernist hard line, and gigantic unpractical sheet formats. Imagination itself was conceived of as a site of liberation.

But the etchings also create a temporal illusion that they have been produced in the past, which contradicted the dominant directives on the historical time of architecture. The reinvigoration of history represented by the use of classical architectural forms, and further perfected in the antiquated watercolour drawings – which emphasise minute architectural and scenic details – essentially highlighted the blind spots of the 'technocratic regime'. In the work of the 'paper architects', dissent was articulated by a certain exuberance of creativity, perhaps an ironic exaggeration of the notion of freedom. Their activities were not primarily directed towards the removal – or even the reform – of a regime, but rather towards the expansion of a sphere of autonomous action. Such explorations into the freedom of 'inner exile' are part of the possible spectrum of gestures of dissent and political efficiency through architecture.[2]

Iskander R Galimov
and Olga Y Galimova,
Taj Mahal City,
1990–91

Galimov and Galimova's drawings dive into a fantasy world where iconic structures seem, at closer sight, to be composed of numerous historical buildings, opening up ever-new reconstructions of an imaginary past. Here, the figure of the Taj Mahal seems both carved into a shattered rock while giving the outline of a city of historic monuments.

The escape into an 'internal world' presented a form of refusal to accept the functionalist environment of socialism.

Anna Luise Schubert,
Documenting the House
on Michaelerplatz,
Vienna (1911),
'Stealing Spaces: The Digital
Reconstruction of Modernism',
Centre for Documentary
Architecture,
Bauhaus–Universität Weimar,
Germany,
2017

Adolf Loos was famously convinced that his interiors could not be truthfully represented through photographs. Perhaps he used various types of marble, wood, brass, mirrors and textures in them to counter the camera's gaze. In photogrammetry, reflective surfaces make it almost impossible to reconstruct a room as a three-dimensional space.

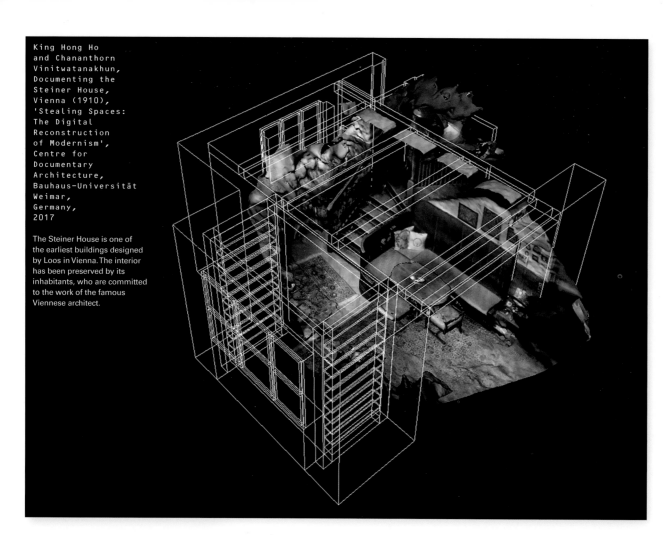

King Hong Ho
and Chananthorn
Vinitwatanakhun,
Documenting the
Steiner House,
Vienna (1910),
'Stealing Spaces:
The Digital
Reconstruction
of Modernism',
Centre for
Documentary
Architecture,
Bauhaus-Universität
Weimar,
Germany,
2017

The Steiner House is one of
the earliest buildings designed
by Loos in Vienna. The interior
has been preserved by its
inhabitants, who are committed
to the work of the famous
Viennese architect.

Barbora Tothova and María Diego,
Photogrammetry of a niche with a
bust of Adolf Loos, Scheu House,
Vienna (1912/13), 'Stealing Spaces:
The Digital Reconstruction of
Modernism', Centre for Documentary
Architecture, Bauhaus-Universität
Weimar, Germany, 2017

Adolf Loos's clients usually had a friendly
relationship with the architect. The lawyer and local
politician Gustav Scheu and his wife even had a bust
of Loos in their living room.

Anna Luise Schubert,
Documenting the Moller House,
Vienna (1927),
'Stealing Spaces: The Digital Reconstruction of Modernism',
Centre for Documentary Architecture,
Bauhaus-Universität Weimar,
Germany,
2017

In summer 2017, the Centre for Documentary Architecture team was invited
to meet the Israeli Ambassador, the Moller House's current resident.

From Documentary Mode to Speculative Future

We could say there are two temporalities existing in architectural representation. On the one hand there are those things that exist – a mapping of the building, the courtyards, and everything that exists in the city, captured in all sorts of documentary media: drawings, mappings, photography or satellite imagery. And on the other hand, out of that, there is the first line that crosses a threshold, a very important threshold, from the past to the future. It is projected from past to future, it interrupts the documentary mode, but exists against its backdrop – as if the rendering is embedded in a photograph, or a documentary and projective mode are flattened into an image. The freedom of creativity might be located on that line from the past into the future along which an analysis erupts into a proposal. Karl Marx argued that the study of history is the motor of politics, political change and revolution. But history is always bound to its techniques, to its historiography and means of narrating, presenting and understanding the past – the particulars of which can lead to a different speculative future. New modes of digital reproduction, 3D scanning and printing technology show how the notion of reproduction, which could potentially lead to mass production, is developed alongside experiments in conservation. Concepts of large-scale architectural production, seriality, replication and systematicity resonate with attempts to record, restore and replicate unique objects and architectures due for preservation. At points even, it seems, the tenets of reproduction, of its mechanisation and digitalisation, come to support not the kind of modernism of erasure, but the old-fashioned conservational techniques. If the future can be folded into such a retrospective analysis, we also begin to re-inhabit a terrain in the past that opens to new meanings, contextualisations and ideas. The future – whether articulated in a utopian novel or outlined in a simple plan – is always a projection into the past.

A recent research experiment with a group of young researchers at the CDA aimed to understand buildings as documentary resources, and as entry-points to comprehend the complex geopolitical and cultural history within which the architecture, the architect, the inhabitant and the architecture's trustees are entangled. Through a series of 'object biographies' of buildings by the architect Adolf Loos in Vienna – certainly one of the most researched sites in architectural history and a classic for architects' design training – the project and exhibition 'Stealing Spaces: The Digital Reconstruction of Modernism' attempted to document the condition of the houses Loos once designed between the 1910s and late 1920s, but also their transformation and changing ownership. Rather than producing a survey of the complete building, architectural details and fragments appeared to contain the seeds of understanding some of the 'deep memory' of the building. As if reversing the mnemotechnics of the interiors which had inscribed the stories into its materiality, the observation of fragments revealed what the documentary filmmaker Patrick Keiller described in his 2010 film *Robinson in Ruins* as 'the molecular basis of historical events', as a 'way to see into the future'.

Proximate Sensing and Digital Tactility

The documentation used photogrammetry – a technique that can generate 3D objects from still photography. The technique of 3D scanning is presently used for architectural surveys with scanners that can capture the details of objects and buildings down to a fraction of a millimetre, or drones that can capture the massing of cities. Yet, here it was used as a form of proximate sensing – to distinguish it from the remote sensing provided by drones

and satellites – conducted, despite the limitations, with hand-held smartphones and other simple cameras. In capturing the sight, the sound of hundreds of shutters of the cameras closing seemed intrusive, and – in the same way as early 19th-century photographers were suspected of 'stealing the soul', turning persons into things – these documentations felt like 'stealing spaces'.

Yet the residents visited during this project were rather moved by the almost haptic approach to photography – zooming in to the level of the grain – and opened to tell the story of the building, of the details and elements within it, with the stories of their lives. Some of the original owners were forced into exile, some were murdered, but each one left a personal trace that could be recorded and interpreted.

Another intention of this collection of object biographies was to capture some 'samples' of Loos's architecture in order to investigate the complexity of copying and reproduction techniques; but also, in engaging with these techniques, to reconstruct both some of the fascination Loos had in the materiality of his buildings, and the historical relations that have inscribed themselves within the captured details. Some of Loos's buildings, such as the Josephine Baker House in Paris that he designed in 1928, remained unfinished. An architectural re-enactment of the house as part of the Ordos 100 project in 2008, proposed by the author of this article, opened the path to multiple trajectories that explored the architectural copy as media. It was this gap between the unfinished plan and the existing oeuvre of Loos's architectures that necessitated answering both to the legal, historical and design questions that such undertaking for copying, or realising an apparently well-known architectural project, posed.

Anna Luise Schubert,
Consulting the Albertina Archive,
Vienna,
'Stealing Spaces: The Digital
Reconstruction of Modernism',
Centre for Documentary Architecture,
Bauhaus-Universität Weimar,
Germany,
2017

Only a few detailed construction drawings are preserved in the archive. The reason might partly be that Loos did not produce many drawings, instead making decisions on site during the construction process. They might also have been lost when Loos decided to go to Paris and asked his collaborators to destroy his archive of plans.

An architectural re-enactment of the house as part of the Ordos 100 project in 2008 opened the path to multiple trajectories that explored the architectural copy as media.

Anna Luise Schubert and Amelie Wegener, Photogrammetry of cello cupboard in the music room, Moller House, Vienna (1927), 'Stealing Spaces: The Digital Reconstruction of Modernism', Centre for Documentary Architecture, Bauhaus–Universität Weimar, Germany, 2017

The interior is impeccably restored to its original state, with only the difference in height between the dining room and the music room, which formed a kind of stage, transformed into a wide staircase.

Ortrun Bargholz, Exhibition view, 'Stealing Spaces: The Digital Reconstruction of Modernism', Centre for Documentary Architecture, Bauhaus–Universität Weimar, Germany, 2017

In a darkened space, the exhibition showed reproductions of selected details of interiors designed by Adolf Loos. Virtual-reality technologies and sound recordings created an immersive environment in which visitors could experience the space and the memories connected by its materiality.

Both the preservation and the documentation of objects are not only acts of protection and safeguarding; rather, they offer new spaces of creative freedom and intervention.

Legally, questions regarding the right to copy this building 75 years after the death of the author in 1933 – the maximum time span that according to international copyright conventions would protect the copyright of authors – opened to research to investigate the 'three lives of modernism'.[3] But the gaps between the existing elaboration of Loos's design for the Josephine Baker House – which is documented only in a 1:33 model, and two different sets of plans in a scale of 1:200 that were inked by his assistant Kurt Unger – and the project to build it in 1:1 also brought about new questions about the details of the design, which seemed closely tied to the relation between Loos and the singer and performer Josephine Baker, as well as to Loos's own sensitivity to the acoustics of space.[4] If Loos, who at the end of his life suffered almost complete deafness, had had the chance to realise the Josephine Baker House in Paris, he would have been forced to refer to a memorised repertoire of design elements and an acoustic catalogue of materials. As such, CDA's reconstruction project re-enacted Loos's *Wohnungswanderungen* (apartment walks) – with which the architect conducted highly didactic tours concentrating not on the entirety of his projects and its meaning, but rather on the materials that were brought together to compose them, as well as on their origins and the architectural details that hold them together.

The room assembled in an installation was not a reconstruction but rather an 'architectural fantasy' assembled from 'digital samples' photogrammetrically scanned from different buildings, reproduced in 1:1 scale and animated through virtual-reality technologies and sound. Each detail or material composition became a starting point for different narratives: interviews with former and contemporary inhabitants, archivists, preservationists and trustees spring out of physical elements, reflecting on the history and afterlife of the architect's work. Put together, the room recomposed the trajectories of object-biographies in a process of endless migration.

In the same way as Loos had pointed to certain details of his work during his apartment walks, these object-biographies could be considered less as copies, and more as samples of possible futures. The process of documenting and copying carries with it the traces of the passage of time, which inevitably transforms the original. Similarly to how preservationists struggle to identify the original, copyists likewise struggle to weigh the pristine state of an imaginary original with its existing version. Both the preservation and the documentation of objects (each of which sometimes involves copying) are not only acts of protection and safeguarding; rather, they offer new spaces of creative freedom and intervention. ∆

Notes
1. Ines Weizman, 'Dissidence Through Architecture', in Kurt Evans, Iben Falconer and Ian Mills (eds), *Perspecta 45: Agency*, MIT Press (Cambridge, MA), 2012, pp 27–38.
2. Ines Weizman (ed), *Architecture and the Paradox of Dissidence*, Routledge (London), 2014.
3. Ines Weizman, 'The Three Lives of Modern Architecture: Wills, Copyrights and their Violations', in Thordis Arrhenius *et al* (eds), *Place and Displacement: Exhibiting Architecture*, Lars Müller (Zurich), 2014, pp 183–96.
4. Ines Weizman, 'Tuning Into the Void: The Aurality of Adolf Loos's Architecture', *Harvard Design Magazine: Did You Read Me?*, 38, 2014, pp 8–16.

Sarah Wigglesworth

unlocking Pentonville

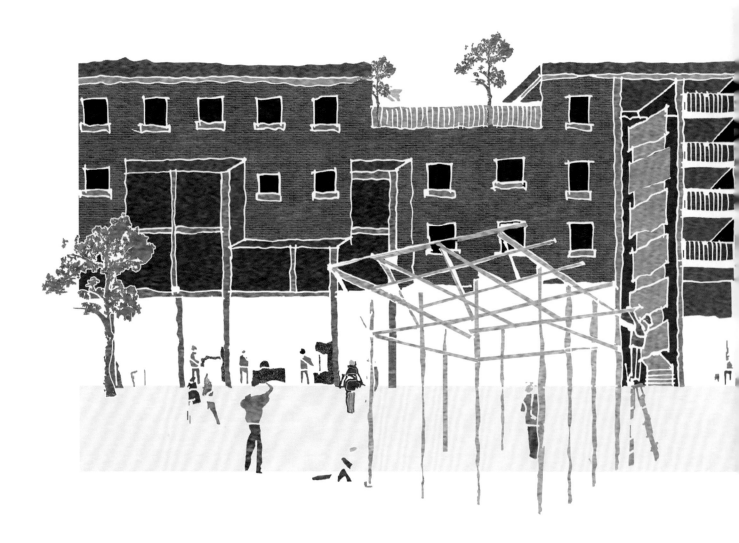

Architectural Liberation in Self-Initiated Projects

Sarah Wigglesworth Architects,
Unlocking Pentonville,
London,
2017

Concept sketch for the proposal, which explores
how the heritage prison buildings can be
redeemed through design interventions aimed
at the wellbeing of the local community.

Capital-driven development is causing an adversarial atmosphere in built-environment planning. Architects often find themselves walking a tightrope between their clients' demands and their own professional imperative to work for the good of the community. But challenging a client on ethics can mean losing work. To improve the situation all round, London-based architect **Sarah Wigglesworth** advocates involving architects at an earlier stage in the planning process, and also encourages her peers to initiate projects themselves to spur debate and potential collaboration. Her practice's urban regeneration proposal centred on a historic prison building in one of the UK's most deprived neighbourhoods serves as an example.

Architecture and planning create the setting in which civic life is played out. Yet on the whole the public realm and the quality of our buildings come about through the instruments of capital. As agents of those commissioning buildings, architects and planners are inherently caught between two potentially conflicting concerns: to satisfy the client's wishes on the one hand, and to answer to their discipline's societal contract on the other. The notion of impartial service to society is embedded not only in the very definition of professionalism, but also explicitly in the Architects' Registration Board (ARB) 'Architects' Code', and in clause 3.1 of the Royal Institute of British Architects (RIBA) 'Code of Professional Conduct'. This states that the architect should 'have a proper concern and due regard for the effect that their work may have on its users and the local community', and should 'be aware of the environmental impact of their work'. Note that nothing stronger than 'awareness' is now required.

Over the course of my career, the balance between societal and personal gain has shifted. Training in the late 1970s and early 1980s, it was still understood that working for the benefit of society was our ethical goal. In the UK, local authority architects' departments carried out impressive work, and experimentation was sanctioned through sponsorship by the public purse. This era saw the invention of innovative spatial typologies, and the emergence of Matrix (representing women's views on the built environment) and the community architecture movement. Some flagship schemes included the redevelopment of two of London's historic markets in Spitalfields and Covent Garden, the building of new forms of housing across London, and ambitious infrastructure projects such as the Thames Barrier at Woolwich, which prevents East and Central London being flooded by storm surges and very high tides.

Since the premiership of Margaret Thatcher and the growth of globalisation, the role of the state has been demonised and its reach eroded. The experimentation that was funded publicly is now under both critical review and development pressure. Despite their well-publicised problems, which originate partly from poor maintenance and flawed policies of housing allocation, politicians are calling for the regeneration of 'failing' 1970s social housing estates such as the Heygate and Aylesbury in South London, and the demolition of unloved buildings such as the Brutalist Robin Hood Gardens (1972) in Poplar, East London, designed by Alison and Peter Smithson. A new caution is in the air, with housing in particular solidifying into typologies based on historical archetypes such as mansion blocks, terraced houses and Tyneside flats. There is a shift away from the Corbusian model of large towers in parkland settings and Radburn layouts towards an urbanism with an emphasis on 'place-making' – the creation of identity in the public realm based on streets and squares, clear demarcations of public and private space, private gardens or balconies as amenity space, and familiar materials such as brick cladding – what in the capital is becoming known as the 'new London vernacular'. Here, the need for social housing under current funding regimes has meant London is both rising in height and cost while simultaneously being hollowed out as private housing is bought by absentee owners living abroad. With legislation leaning in favour of developers, and the reduced power of local authority planning departments

Sarah Wigglesworth
Architects,
Proposal for the
conversion of Robin
Hood Gardens,
London, 2011

below: This speculative work
considers how the system-built
concrete construction of Robin
Hood Gardens, an iconic social
housing estate in East London
designed by Alison
and Peter Smithson and
completed in 1972, could be
amended to provide a wider
range of apartments more
suited to the needs of the large
families currently occupying the
two- and three-bedroom flats.
It also looks at ways to improve
the environmental conditions
within the deck-access blocks.

Hans Peter
(Felix) Trenton,
Aylesbury Estate,
Walworth,
London,
1977

opposite: Covering a huge site
between Walworth and the Old
Kent Roads in South London, at
its height the Aylesbury Estate
comprised 2,700 homes, housing
close to 10,000 people. Since the
late 1990s there have been plans
for comprehensive redevelopment.
Work finally began in 2010 and
is planned to continue in several
stages until 2032, eventually
replacing the estate's social
housing with 3,500 new homes,
50 per cent of which are expected
to be affordable with the rest for
private sale.

to deal with this imbalance, the question is begged: whose responsibility is it to uphold civic values?

At the institutional level, the ARB (established by Parliament to regulate the profession in the UK) is focused predominantly on the 'consumer' of architectural services in demanding that architects have appropriate training and insurance, and on the misuse by practitioners of the title 'architect'. The RIBA has periodic and recurring anxiety about architects' ethical position, but its message is as incoherent as its remit, and reflects prevailing dogmas. While purporting to safeguard architectural knowledge and upholding the social contract, the RIBA behaves sycophantically to government and the agents of big business, generally turning a blind eye to ethical abuses and the bad behaviour of its members while sanctioning the vanity of its more famous public figures. The absence of a clear ethical position by the bodies that represent architects in society brings all of the profession into disrepute, and does not provide a positive narrative around which we could cohere.

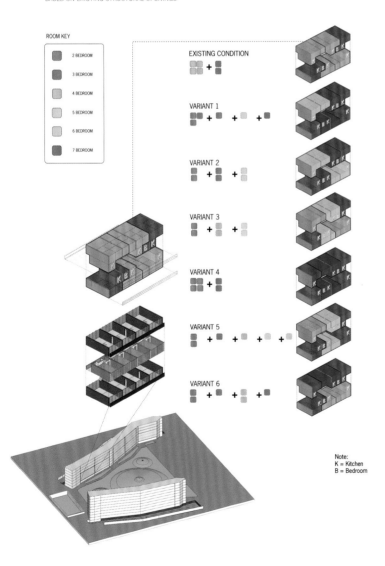

POSSIBLE BEDROOM PERMUTATIONS
BASED ON EXISTING STRUCTURAL OPENINGS

ROBIN HOOD GARDENS RE-VISIONS

ROOM KEY

2 BEDROOM
3 BEDROOM
4 BEDROOM
5 BEDROOM
6 BEDROOM
7 BEDROOM

EXISTING CONDITION

VARIANT 1

VARIANT 2

VARIANT 3

VARIANT 4

VARIANT 5

VARIANT 6

Note:
K = Kitchen
B = Bedroom

Sarah Wigglesworth Architects
and Jeremy Till,
9/10 Stock Orchard Street,
London,
2000

Designed, funded and occupied by Sarah
Wigglesworth and her partner Jeremy Till,
the experimental Stock Orchard Street project
explores new models of sustainable living and
working in inner London and 'green' material
expression. A passive environmental envelope,
it employs recycled and crop-based materials.

Locating Liberation

Architects and planners face difficult choices in dealing with these changes. The first point to make is that everyone involved in building operates within the same political and economic framework, and room for manoeuvre is restricted on all sides. The large, successful practices are good at aligning themselves with their influential clients and navigating away from ethical problems. The smaller firms have less to lose, but they understand that it is commercial suicide to bite the hand that feeds them. Most architects are treading a fine line trying to uphold their principles while working within the parameters that allow building to take place at all.

In a highly competitive business, architects have to be realistic about where their work comes from. Challenging clients on their ethics means potentially losing work. As a result it is rare to find an architect candid enough to debate either the system or the manner in which buildings are procured, much less criticise a client. For example, before demolition was made inevitable, my own firm – Sarah Wigglesworth Architects – was effectively blacklisted by the developer of the Robin Hood Gardens site for carrying out a pro-bono feasibility study on behalf of the Twentieth Century Society (an organisation that campaigns for the safeguarding of 20th-century British architecture) that they viewed as challenging their project, as it aimed to show that the estate could be upgraded environmentally and converted into larger flats meeting the needs of the families that were crowded into unfit accommodation.

Accordingly, critical architecture is confined to academia, where dispassionate, independent examination of issues is encouraged and where there is a client-free environment. Interestingly, the focus in a number of schools is now on work that aims to engage with communities, to empower them through knowledge, language and action to hold to account those responsible for the built environment visited upon them. This has resulted in the emergence of 'live projects' in which teams of students work with such groups to offer their design, management, communication, planning and building skills, learning to provide services similar to those they will use later in practice. Whether or not this genuinely challenges the ethics of conventional practice, or merely co-opts naive but willing students into unpaid labour, is debatable. What seems clear, though, is that this is a reaction to the unrelenting narrative of capitalism played out in practice and the desire to spread access to architecture's ways of knowing and doing into sectors of the community that are affected by our work, but rarely involved in its briefing and processes. Academia has perhaps become the only place where this is possible.

Many of those interested in the built environment, and especially architects, seek a critique of the effects that global capital is having on our cities, a better understanding of how finance controls development, and how land supply and planning issues come together to create the environment making up our rural areas, towns and cities. However, there does not appear to be any school of architecture in the UK that situates its work within this context and gives students the skills to navigate the realities of development with a good grounding in land economy. Isolated from the practice context and with little knowledge of its conditions and

Sarah Wigglesworth Architects,
Unlocking Pentonville,
London, 2017

above: Part of the Caledonian Road panorama showing the prison in the context of its surroundings on both sides of the road.

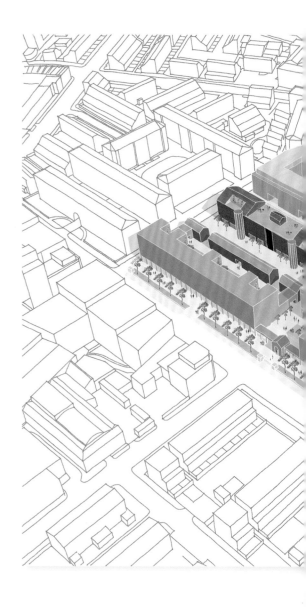

below: The proposal in its local context. The coloured area represents the city block occupied by the prison on Caledonian Road (which crosses diagonally from lower right to top left). The entire complex is reconfigured as a neighbourhood supporting intergenerational housing, live/work and creative spaces, including a School of Creative Arts. The scheme preserves the heritage value of the prison buildings, based on recognition of the cellular spaces within and the long vistas down the central corridors. As a symbolic strategy, a new public square is placed in the centre of the scheme, replacing the all-seeing vantage point of the original prison conception.

drivers, it is unlikely that architectural academics will invent new processes and financial models that could potentially change the status quo.

This leaves architects interested in breaking free from these constraints with an interesting dilemma: where and how can agency be achieved and how could this alter current conditions?

One method my firm has experimented with is to carry out projects where the agenda is initiated and driven by us. By doing so we hope to engage new audiences and generate debate so as to influence the outcomes of development. In the majority of our projects we are invited on board once the development parameters (density, land price, market context, planning brief, building standards and so on) have been established by others. What this leaves for the architect is then relatively restricted, and often provides great challenges, such as trying to break down the mass of a very large building by visually 'reducing' the bulk of a proposal. If architects were invited to participate earlier in the decision making on matters of spatial organisation, appropriate density or material expression, and there were open debate that included the local community, this would be more likely to create a more interesting, meaningful and responsive built environment, and one that is less adversarial.

Escaping Architectural Confinement
Unlocking Pentonville (2017) illustrates the idea and is in the tradition of the self-initiated research-led projects that started in 1995 with my own house and office at 9/10 Stock Orchard Street in Islington, North London. A speculative project initiated and carried out by Sarah Wigglesworth Architects, it focuses on Pentonville Prison, which is situated less than a mile from our office. While based on a real, timely situation, it aims to tackle the problem of social exclusion that results in serial incarceration from a spatial organisation and socioeconomic perspective, with the wellbeing of residents and the local community in mind rather than being the product of financial calculations and policy fulfilment. Moreover, as it involves the potential reinvention of the prison site, it engages ideas of freedom and social justice, and the role of the built environment in securing these for everyone.

above: The new square with the Chapel (with radio mast and showing a movie) at its centre, and a cafe/flower shop to the right. The School of Creative Arts is far left.

below: Section showing the Caledonian Road on the left and the converted prison buildings on the right. Left to right: general needs and older people's housing over workshops and retail spaces; workshop courtyard and two-storey live/work; service yard; converted prison buildings including live/work preserving the gallery arrangement of the existing prison on the ground and first floors.

The intention is to open up and reveal the existing historic structures, offering opportunities to remember and learn from the prison's past

right: Unlocking Pentonville public exhibition, June 2017. The exhibition invited the public to view the research and the proposal and leave comments, and was accompanied by a mini-series of three debates around issues of Memory, Equality and Justice, and Wellbeing.

Her Majesty's Prison Service is selling its inner-city jails, releasing these sites for redevelopment. The area is subject to pressure from the nearby King's Cross development, a 27-hectare (67-acre) new urban quarter currently being constructed on the site of former railway lands north of King's Cross and St Pancras stations in London. Taking into account local concerns around housing and its affordability, and in view of Pentonville Prison's history and the listed status of some of its buildings, the challenge was to envision a new life for the site that communicates its past and considers its relevance for the future. Unlocking Pentonville therefore imagines a radical new vision for this area of Caledonian Road in North London.

Completed in 1842, Pentonville served as a model for many other British prisons and is still operational. It is a Category B/C Local Prison serving the surrounding population, and also holds remand prisoners and some longer-term inmates. Colonel Joshua Jebb's design was based on two key ideas: individual confinement using the separate cell system (each cell measures 4.1 x 2.3 metres/13.5 x 7.5 feet) and surveillance along the arms of the radial plan. Originally designed to hold 520 prisoners, it now houses 1,264 as a result of extensions and additions to the original five wings. Violence, including murders, have taken place within its walls.

It costs over £30,000 per annum to keep someone in a Category B/C prison like Pentonville.[1] Questions therefore arise as to who is criminalised and which crimes are most likely to lead to imprisonment. The London Borough of Islington has one of the highest crime rates and youth reoffending rates in London. Although crime occurs across all sections of society, young people, ethnic minorities and those living in poverty are more likely to end up in prison. The Caledonian Ward, in which the prison is located, is one of the most deprived in the UK and the most deprived in Islington, with very high densities, poorer than average educational and skills attainment, access to open space and healthcare, higher levels of obesity and shorter life expectancy than national averages. High housing costs are a primary cause of inequality. Public-sector cuts and welfare reforms are exacerbating these trends.

The Pentonville prison site presents a unique opportunity to respond to these complex social, physical and historical contexts. The aim of the Unlocking Pentonville project is to configure a new neighbourhood that breaks down the prison walls connecting the site and the surrounding streets, and replaces the all-seeing perspectival surveillance point at the focus of the radial arms with a new public space at the heart of the site. The intention is to open up and reveal the existing historic structures, offering opportunities to remember and learn from the prison's past while redeeming the buildings for new uses relevant to a post-prison future.

The proposal consists of a range of multi-generational housing with sizes and values related to income and facilities for education and training that could potentially help reduce crime and reoffending. At the foundation of this work is a desire to create a socially just neighbourhood, with improved access to local health advice and fitness facilities alongside new public spaces, gardens and community buildings that contribute to an increased sense of wellbeing in order to make a place that uses creativity (and the self-definition that arises from this) as a thread that binds together all the activities proposed for the site. For example, a crèche staffed by local people and assisted by third-agers feeds a School of Creative Arts that educates children through an arts-based curriculum, and will form a feeder for local colleges. Along the Caledonian Road, four storeys of apartments (both general needs and for older people) sit over maker spaces and retail outlets serviced by a makers' yard and live/work units to the rear. The prison buildings are variously converted into housing and workshop spaces, retaining their former identity but with reconfigured fenestration, roof profiles and elements of their interiors. To the northeast corner of the site, a youth centre and sport facilities would occupy a converted prison wing.

The listed Chapel remains at the heart of the proposal, facing the new public square, but is repurposed as a community building, radio station and, at ground level, a market. Its east wall can serve as an outdoor cinema screen viewed from deck chairs in the square. A cafe and flower shop occupy the northeast corner of the square, behind which the ruined facade of the former prison hosts a vertical garden, with more live/work and growing beds occupying the footprint of the ghost cells.

Unlocking Pentonville was showcased at a public exhibition in an empty shop on Caledonian Road during June 2017, accompanied by three debates on the themes of Memory, Equality and Justice, and Wellbeing. The event was well attended and elicited a great deal of interest from the community who offered their opinions on the future of the site and comments on the proposal. It provided an opportunity to engage politicians, local people and opinion-formers in a debate about the potential future of the neighbourhood – an important aspect of the proposal. The hope is that with the freedom to make proposals before the economic parameters are set, it becomes possible to explore the spatial, economic and cultural agendas of such sites at a stage when people can see how ambitious a development could be, and we can influence the way we renew our cities. By clearly showing the links between crime and social justice, Unlocking Pentonville challenges the notion of 'best value' as the highest price paid for the land, and shows that social justice and equality, stable communities and beauty also have a value, if only we could recognise it. ⌁

Note

1. Ministry of Justice, 'Costs per prison place and cost per prisoner by individual prison establishment', National Offender Management Service Annual Report and Accounts 2015–16, 27 October 2016: www.gov.uk/government/statistics/prison-performance-statistics-2015-to-2016.

ScottWhitbyStudio,
Courtyard therapy space,
Simon Community,
London,
2016

Working with and trying to
understand the therapeutic
needs of one of London's oldest
homeless communities helped
ScottWhitbyStudio to find
ways to create private spaces
of contemplation as part of the
refurbishment of Simon's London
home. The project has recently
achieved planning permission.

The Freedom of Being Three

The Art of Architectural Growing Up

Experiential learning and an open, enquiring mind are as integral to the profession of architecture as they are to a child's development. Watching his daughter in her early years, **Alex Scott-Whitby** has noticed parallels with the evolution of his practice. Founded in the year she was born, his London architecture and urban design consultancy ScottWhitbyStudio has gone through similar phases: from the seed of an idea, to finding its feet, to seeking guidance from its forebears, to pushing boundaries.

My architectural studio is the same age as my three-year-old daughter, and this matters. Watching the freedom a child has to learn and develop is one of life's great pleasures and has changed my outlook on life and work completely. It has given me a language for understanding the processes of creativity that come through curiosity, unknowing, and joyful but purposeful exploration. For me, child development mirrors that of my practice, allowing me the freedom to adopt an innocence and youthful approach to the work knowing that at the right time and in the right way, we will grow up.

Conception

The conception of setting up independently comes to many of us particularly when we are working for others. We flirt with the idea, court allies and even engage in disastrous flings outside of our current parameters. We then either couple up or go it alone. And here begins the gestation. For some this time is elephantine; for others it will be completed over tea. For me it was reasonably quick, which made support incredibly important. I understood that I needed to know the limits of my competence so I looked to others to help steer a path. These were people in practices or businesses who offered wisdom and warmth to the kernel of ideas knowing that those fragile, infantile thoughts were worth nourishing.

Alex Scott-Whitby,
Lyra's Shadow,
2015

Standing on two feet at an early age can sometimes be difficult, but once you get going there is no stopping you.

ScottWhitbyStudio, Riyadh Villa,
Diriyah, Saudi Arabia, 2014

below: The studio's first commission was the design of a private villa and estate. Currently under construction, the 12,500-square-metre (134,500-square-foot) project looks to learn from the region's vernacular to create a new screen wall that dapples light during the day and emits it at night.

ScottWhitbyStudio,
Caution Cinema,
various dockside locations,
UK,
2016–

Caution Cinema is an immersive alien yet comforting experience for the UK's dockworkers. More than 1,000 acoustic cones create an anechoic chamber within a 6 x 2 metre (20 x 6 feet) shipping container. The project was completed in 2016 and has been on tour ever since.

Birth

And then, at 40,000 feet (12,000 metres) on a flight back to London following a meeting with one such supporter, the studio was born. In the first months I stood still, staring awestruck at the world I was now inhabiting. I was surrounded by caring and invested individuals prepared to help, but ultimately unable to do what I needed to. At this early stage, as with infants, there was an element of luck. We found clients who were prepared to take a risk and were excited by the prospect of learning and growing with us; going on a journey together. There is a freedom in going to clients with a portfolio that bears no relevance to the brief they are asking you to meet. They see your potential rather than evaluating your past.

Sitting Up

As the practice started to grow we learned to sit up and to exercise our voice, though speaking a language only we could understand. The world was the right way up and we had got through the dangerous early months unscathed, if a little broke. A child's brain is designed to absorb anything and everything that it can; it does not yet know what is important to retain so all information is given equal weight. Over time, the child discriminates what is important, consolidates key skills and then specialises in certain areas; naivety is advantageous. As a studio we aim to nurture this childlike curiosity in our projects. We say yes to a wide range of briefs that interest and excite us, especially with clients who value this fresh perspective and flexible way of thinking.

ScottWhitbyStudio,
St Peter's Cheap
Churchyard
renewal project,
City of London,
2017

With the Corporation of London, the studio is currently working on a detailed design to rejuvenate the site of a former church, burnt down in the Fire of London, into an urban pocket park.

ScottWhitbyStudio,
Victoria Tower,
Westminster,
London, 2015

Working with the client, an
international property developer,
the architects proposed a double-
ordered 18-storey, 140-unit
residential tower next to Victoria
station. The facade is inspired by
the archways of its neighbours:
Westminster Cathedral and
Victoria Station.

Learning to Walk

But this comes at a cost. Children are not self-sufficient and certainly unable to meet their own basic needs. As a business in those formative days the freedom to explore also came with its own pitfalls: managing staff; the payroll at the end of each month; the search for other projects while busy juggling those we already had; and giving directions when you are not sure yourself of the road to take. But I suppose like any toddler when they start to walk, they have to run, and when they do they tend to pass between two safe and comforting pairs of hands. Importantly, when a young child falls over they do not have that far to fall; they fear less about making mistakes, and generally those around them celebrate the mistakes that happen. These are salutary lessons for us as a practice as we try to push the boundaries in everything we do.

Sitting Up On the Shoulders of Giants

As we have grown up we have started to talk and walk more confidently, we have tested our ideas and explored our own way of thinking. From the design of a cinema in a shipping container to a tower in London, we have begun to establish a rhythm to our work. Our library in the studio is full of monographs by those who are older and wiser than us, whom we still use for inspiration and in some cases mimicry. My grandfather (George Whitby) was an architect, and on his bookshelf was a very weathered copy of the complete works of Edwin Lutyens. Before starting any design with his business partner Donald McMoran he would apparently ask: 'What would Lutyens do?'

Learning From Others

I find it amazing that some new practices emerge from their architectural parents fully formed, as experts practising the methods and language of their teachers, able to know what their forefathers/mothers would do and seamlessly re-create. Despite having the best teachers, I could not have done this. We have needed to cultivate our own culture and language symbiotically through more than 40 projects and some seriously experiential learning. We debunked to a church for 10 days to better understand its inner workings; we completed soup runs to support the homeless community for whom we were designing a new home; we have travelled the world to better understand our clients' influences and inspirations. These processes change us, but also change our clients' perspectives, allowing shared dialogue that cuts to the very heart of design.

Being Three

We are now happy to be three years old. We have tantrums, but we are learning our own mind and have become architecturally conversant. Our projects are getting more grown up: a redevelopment and enhancement plan for a Grade II-listed chapel in Westminster capable of holding 2,000 people; an office building for a FTSE 100 company, and a new public square outside St Paul's Cathedral for the City of London. We still rely on the wisdom of others and have to know when to listen and learn. We are free being three and maybe this is where we should remain. ⌂

ScottWhitbyStudio, Inhabited Section, Westminster Chapel, London, 2017–27

Immersing themselves within the workings of a Grade II-listed chapel next to Buckingham Palace helped the studio to devise a 10-year strategy of renewal for a forgotten Victorian masterpiece. The first phase is due for completion in 2019.

Anupama Kundoo Architects,
Volontariat Homes for Homeless
Children,
Pondicherry,
India,
2008

Baked-in-situ mud structures involve the
construction of domes and vaulted forms
in unbaked mud bricks and mud mortar,
which are then fired in place for three to
four days until they are converted into
ceramic. Fire is the cement that stabilises
the structure, making it water-resistant.

Freedom from the Known

Anupama Kundoo

Imagining the Future Without the Baggage of the Past

As a newly qualified female architect in early 1990s India, **Anupama Kundoo**'s first instinct was to seek to live as independently and lightly as possible – and to help others to do likewise. A self-build project intended to be temporary turned into a lifestyle, and led to a career focused on engaging local workers in eco-minded building that marries new technology with familiar materials. Now based in Madrid, she describes her journey so far, including her own built work and her doctoral studies of a project involving mud dwellings fired to permanence when fully built.

Architecture, a backdrop for human life, has always expressed the state of society and its values. Architecture is considered to have a capacity to improve people's lives, and the role of the architect has traditionally been regarded as a visionary one that can steer an evolving society forward, through shaping the spaces in which people spend their time individually and collectively. However, in the rapidly changing current landscape, the production of architecture is greatly influenced by an industrialised building trade rather than the other way round, and there is increasing concern about the architect's diminishing role in shaping the built environment.

This is very worrying as we live in turbulent times, with major challenges ranging from climate change concerns and rapid urbanisation to environmental degradation and migration, to name a few. Current ways of developing cities and infrastructure and constructing buildings are creating more environmental, social and economic imbalances, and more problems than they solve. Architects have the capacity to synthesise diverse concerns into holistic projects, and the architect's role is more relevant than ever. The future needs to be designed holistically, rather than be developed piecemeal as a result of various trends and habits which are clearly not sustainable. 'Freedom from the Known'[1] is perhaps the best way to summarise the approach that could lead to innovations and new prototypes for humankind's future built environment through integrated thinking.

I grew up in Bombay and graduated as an architect 28 years ago. Quite untypical for a young Indian girl, I immediately moved out of my parents' apartment into my own. I preferred to be self-reliant and take the responsibility for the consequences of my own life's choices, as I did realise very early on that I wanted to live my life motivated by my sense of purpose, choosing adventure rather than my need for security. I worked for a year in Bombay, while figuring out where to go to when I would leave it soon. I landed up in Auroville, an international city-in-the-making in rural Tamil Nadu, intending to camp for a while, and built a thatched hut there for myself. I ended up living in it for over 10 years till I moved to my more permanent Wall House, that I created in its vicinity.

The different aspects of my quest for freedom in both my personal and professional life are reflected in many of my architectural projects, from my first thatched hut and Wall House through to the recent Full Fill homes, the aim of which is freedom from the tyranny of affording housing.

Reducing to the Max

As a fresh architect from Bombay, travelling around in rural India, I was fascinated by the simplicity of shelter in villages. Self-built thatched mud structures housed the bulk of the population. In Auroville, I was struck by the Italian architect Piero Cicionesi's contemporary interpretation of the hut in his collective housing project 'Aspiration' (1971), and the very simple thatched 'capsules' with their triangulated geometry, developed in the next decade by Johnny Allen, an Australian architect influenced by Buckminster Fuller.

Having consciously left Bombay's city life along with the related rat race, I was looking for personal freedom from the need for permanence when it came to shelter. I wanted to live lightly and simply, so that I would liberate my valuable time and face the adventure of life on a day-to-day basis, taking the time to discover what I truly needed. My hut in Petite Ferme (1991), an Auroville community in its outskirts, was influenced by the way several other Aurovilians lived in those pioneering years, and was constructed in a few weeks.

The round wood structure of untreated *Casuarina* trees tied together with coconut rope, stood on rough-cut granite stilts that prevented termites from reaching the wood. The upper floor was of split *pakamaram* palm stems, and woven coconut leaves were the roof finish. The bedroom, a raised platform, was tucked into an alcove, and a sitting hammock hung within another small alcove. Two solar panels took care of the lighting and music; a black plastic bag hung outdoors provided warm water in the colder months, and used shower water fed papaya and banana plants, next to the salad and vegetable garden.

Expecting neither the hut nor my adventure phase to last that long, I spent over 10 long years there while designing permanent houses and public buildings for the others, with a growing concern about achieving climatic comfort naturally, spending resources judiciously, and looking for beauty in simplicity. There was joy in freedom from the need for permanence.

Anupama Kundoo,
Hut in Petite Ferme,
Auroville,
India,
1991

The author had designed herself a simple thatched dwelling where she lived for over 10 years. It represents her personal quest for freedom from material possessions through reducing her needs to the essentials. Time and space for contemplation are essential to creativity and innovation.

Anupama Kundoo,
Hut in Petite Ferme,
Auroville,
India,
1991

The living area is raised on stilts, and constructed in *Casuarina* round wood elements, tied together with coconut rope. Woven coconut leaves serve as thatch, and split *pakamaram* palms are used to finish the floor.

New Building Technologies with Time-Tested Materials

The experience of living in my hut revealed to me that most conventional building technologies, including reinforced-concrete roofs, heated up homes, were costly and energy intensive and excluded local craftsmen. I began investigating preindustrial *achikal* bricks and lime mortar, and developed terracotta roofing elements that could provide a livelihood to local potters who had to compete with the growing metal and plastic industry.

My present 'permanent' home, Wall House (Petite Ferme, Auroville, 2001), is the result of extensive research and experimentation. A long and narrow vaulted space, 2.2 metres (7 feet) wide, contained within the brick masonry accommodates the various activities arranged in a row, as in a train. Activities spill to the northeast into alcoves and projections, and on the southwest, under the large overhang of the main vaulted roof. The design of the house thus ensures that the activities are cocooned into private secure spaces, while the spillover in the living areas is large and open to nature. While simply organised with clearly defined lines and masses, the play in the volumes makes it hard to distinguish where the inside ends and outside begins.

Anupama Kundoo,
Wall House,
Auroville,
India,
2001

above: The architect's own house is built in exposed, locally made preindustrial *achikal* bricks, with terracotta roofing elements. Perforated ferrocement fins were among the technologies tested here for application in other projects. The idea is to reduce dependency on high-energy materials and facilitate the participation of local artisans.

below: Narrow and cosy private spaces transition into larger generous expanding social spaces that seamlessly connect with the nature outdoors.

While simply organised with clearly defined lines and masses, the play in the volumes makes it hard to distinguish where the inside ends and outside begins.

The exposed brick facades set in lime mortar are scaled down by the 2.5-centimetre (1-inch) high *achikal* bricks, which require far less energy than factory bricks. Catenary vaults using custom-made hollow clay tubes are insulating and eliminate the need for structural steel. Vaults in the ground floor use *achikal* bricks structurally. Flat terraces use custom-made trapezoidal modules over partly pre-cast beams as in a jack arch. Terracotta pots are used as fillers on intermediate floors to increase the effective depth of concrete while minimising the volume of concrete and steel.

My doctoral thesis (TU Berlin, 2008), on the rare technology pioneered by Pondicherry-based ceramist Ray Meeker from the mid-1980s until the late 1990s, consists of baking mud houses in situ, after constructing them. In principle a structure built with mud bricks and mud mortar is stuffed with other ceramic products as if it were a kiln, and fired as a whole to achieve the strength of brick. Typically kiln walls absorb about 40 per cent of the heat generated. In this technology, the house is the kiln, and the 'heat loss' is directed towards firing the house and stabilising it from potential water damage. The fuel cost is largely accountable to the products inside. The strength of brick can be achieved for the price of mud. Further, the cement in the mortar mix becomes unnecessary. This technology is labour-intensive with very little need for 'purchased' materials. Thus the money spent remains in the local economy and it enriches it. The house becomes a producer of sustainable building materials instead of being a consumer.

The Volontariat Homes for Homeless Children (2008), at Tuttipakam in Pondicherry, were realised using this technology under Ray Meeker's technical guidance, for the NGO Volontariat. Sixteen homeless children live in an intimate, protected environment with four foster parents in four clusters. The design offers affordable solutions not only in monetary terms but also with regard to all other resources, in the context of a tug-of-war between development and environment. The project radically rethinks affordability in the light of sustainability. The first cluster engaged international master's students of architecture, spreading building knowledge. Cost concerns being a key design consideration, unconventional materials and urban waste are incorporated: bicycle wheel frames as formwork for windows and later as window grilles; glass bottles as masonry units in toilet areas; and glass chai cups to finish the openings at the top of the dome.

Anupama Kundoo Architects,
Volontariat Homes for Homeless Children,
Pondicherry,
India,
2008

Larger catenary domes house four children each and the adjoining smaller domes accommodate the foster parents.

The strength of brick can be achieved for the price of mud. Further, the cement in the mortar mix becomes unnecessary.

Anupama Kundoo Architects,
Unbound: Library of Lost Books,
Barcelona,
Spain,
2014

Empowerment Through Knowledge

To express 'Liberty' at BCN Re.Set, the 300th-year celebration of Catalunya, the pavilion Unbound: Library of Lost Books (2014) in Barcelona was proposed as a place that celebrates reading and expresses freedom as a place where knowledge is free: knowledge is empowerment, and knowledge will lead to progress and freedom.

An 'outdoor' place under the shade of 'trees', where everybody has a memory of reading books, the pavilion is free from the confines of walls of buildings. Books – the 'building blocks' of society – are facing extinction even though the act of reading continues. 'Obsolete' books are rescued from pulping or burning, and recycled as a construction material to build a canopy. Liberation is lightness. These are lightweight structures for heavyweight books that transcend the sense of 'weight' to focus on the perception of the 'light' element of the book: content. Books, made at the environmental cost of trees, are recycled and reconstructed into trees.

Three canopies shade the Salvador Seguí Square through central trunks constructed of steel tubular profiles of varying diameters just like branches. Canopies are made of vacuum-packed books, packaged the same way as delicatessen items like ham and olives, to symbolise the extension of shelf life and create the association of highly valued though familiar objects. These are assembled together and attached to the structure using cable wire.

The colourful book covers can be seen from the aerial view, while the text pages can be seen from below. The rectilinear geometry of the units assembled into circular forms is a continuation from the similar concept of the cobbled paving below.

'Obsolete books' are recycled to create canopies to express the idea that knowledge leads to freedom. Books as objects are facing transition but the act of reading continues. The Library of Lost Books questions the future form of libraries and their role in cities as houses of knowledge at a time of digitalisation.

Anupama Kundoo Architects,
Full Fill Home,
Venice Biennale,
Venice,
Italy,
2016

Full Fill Home is a prototype of prefabricated ferrocement modules that can be assembled within a week. It was aimed at liberating the resident from the tyranny of affording housing, which is a growing global concern, by finding high-speed solutions using significantly less materials.

The voids within the ferrocement units, which are a part of the structural concept, double up to serve as the entire storage system, making additional furniture practically redundant. Ferrocement elements are finished with embedded colour pigments to define voids and highlight the slenderness of the forms.

Bringing Housing Back to the People

Affording housing, and social segregation due to affordability of housing, have emerged as key concerns in cities worldwide. Full-scale prototypes for 'Full Fill Homes' – at Chennai (2014), Auroville (2015) and the Venice Biennale (2016) – were driven by the quest for freedom from the tyranny of affording housing, through building knowledge within the community and empowering people to participate in house construction. They bring housing back to the people, even in the urban context.

Ferrocement – a lightweight, highly resilient material – has yet to be fully exploited in housing production. The stackable modular system offers low-tech yet speedy construction with minimal environmental impact. The voids inside the blocks strengthen the thin elements while becoming the complete storage solution for the homeowner, accommodating even the kitchen sink itself, making furniture redundant. The storage units are emphasised through use of bright colours.

The 2.5-centimetre (1-inch) thick lightweight elements are produced in the backyards of masons' homes, thereby reducing costs, while helping the local economy. Small-diameter steel meshes give tensile strength to the cement, significantly reducing high-embodied-energy materials. These take less than 48 hours to produce, and, after four weeks' curing time, can be assembled in six days.

The Architect and the Personal Sense of Freedom

Architects are generally optimistic and envision how things could be, or ought to be, in the interest of the larger collective. If they are too entangled in present trends themselves, or their personal livelihoods are dependent on market forces, their self-interest could stand in the way, leaving them in a passive role and even performing as puppets in the hands of developers and other drivers. Being pessimistic does not help things, and nor does being so preoccupied with one's own survival that one is obliged to produce projects that are mere repetitions of current habits. In order to remain visionary, then, perhaps architects need first and foremost to be truly free themselves. To sustain a natural way of being that is courageous, demonstrates integrity, and is an expression of the architect's vision and ideals for society, is perhaps then integral to the capacity to envision a better future. When architects can align with their values and act out of such a sense of freedom, even small projects can have a big impact. ⌀

Note
1. The title 'Freedom from the Known' was originally used for selected excerpts from talks by Jiddu Krishnamurti, renowned Indian philosopher, speaker and writer; edited by Mary Lutyens and published by Harper and Row in 1969. It is considered to be the official repository of his authentic teachings.

Kata Fodor

Lessons from Launching an

Atelier Kite,
Hackney Kitchen,
Royal Academy of Arts,
London, 2016

Isometric view of the
Food Palace, combining
supermarket and kitchen
in an indoor public park.

Alternative Architectural Practice

After graduating from an innovative Master's programme at the Royal Danish Academy of Fine Arts in Copenhagen, **Kata Fodor** was not ready for the confines of work in a traditional architecture firm with jobs initiated by clients. Through co-founding the multidisciplinary design studio Atelier Kite, which proactively pitches well-researched ideas to carefully targeted potential clients, she has been able to continue the meaningful engagement she enjoyed as a student. Here she sets out the studio's approach, reflects on the challenges she has faced, and underlines the importance of major cultural institutions in fostering creativity.

Founding a practice after graduation has taught me several lessons over the past years. Our studio, Atelier Kite, is a collaborative platform for architectural activism, but it has also been my way to test the limits of the power and the freedom I possess as an architect in a rapidly changing world and a society facing challenges on all fronts.

Architectural academia tends to cherish ideas of peaceful coexistence between people with each other and with their environment. However, the year I finished architecture school, Europe as a whole seemed to be headed in a different direction; 2015 was loaded with heart-wrenching events, from Charlie Hebdo to the European refugee crisis, rendering most design projects as vain efforts on the sidelines of a society visibly growing less united in every way.

The Luxury of Academia

The prospect of an adult life working in a traditional architectural practice did not appear quite so obvious any more. I had no doubt about architecture's power to shape the future in meaningful ways; I was just not sure architects necessarily accessed that power. Academia is surely in a difficult position in trying to equip future architects for the changing role they can play amid rapid transformations within the profession and in society at large. However, the lack of a paying client, rigid brief and formulated commission are what often enable our most meaningful engagement with complex problems. The luxury of school projects is not that they can be out of touch with reality, but, on the contrary, the chance to work exactly on what seems most relevant at any time.

My conclusion was therefore to stubbornly continue doing what I had been in school in the Urbanism and Societal Change Master's programme at the Royal Danish Academy of Fine Arts, Copenhagen. With a small group of architects and economists, we began to develop the idea of a multidisciplinary collective that could act as our collaborative framework for meaningful projects. We shared a deep frustration regarding society's relationship with the complex environmental, economic and societal challenges to come. And a concern over the prevalent escapism, fear and nostalgia that act as substitutes in a culture short of shared visions for a bright collective future. We set out to work towards such shared visions in whatever scale or format this might be possible. We would initiate our projects based on research, rather than briefs, and – we believed – the relevance of such projects would ultimately find their clients as well.

Endorsement by the Establishment

These bold fantasies actually turned into a reality in late 2015, thanks to a unique opportunity to work with and exhibit at the Royal Academy of Arts (RA) in London. Our very first project, Hackney Kitchen, won the Urban Jigsaw competition, an open call by the RA seeking speculative proposals for London's brownfield sites. The winning projects were not just to be showcased, but also further developed for nearly a year within the RA's Architecture Programme. Being a part of this Urban Jigsaw series, with regular public presentations, talks and a concluding exhibition in 2016, was effectively a form of incubation for us. Furthermore, it meant that a prestigious cultural institution had endorsed our thinking. Suddenly, all reactions became more supportive, relevant stakeholders more accessible, and everyone a bit more committed and willing to put faith in our vision. Developers, architects and journalists started to take an interest in us, and we established Atelier Kite as an alternative design practice. The impact of our RA exposure could not be overstated and exemplifies the larger responsibility of powerful cultural institutions.

Atelier Kite,
Hackney Kitchen,
Royal Academy of Arts,
London,
2016

At an evening organised on the themes of Food and Housing, Atelier Kite invited Dan Hill, Professor Tim Lang and Carolyn Steel to discuss the Hackney Kitchen project.

Hackney Kitchen built on our previous academic work, revisiting Margarete Schütte-Lihotzky's famous Frankfurt kitchen from 1926. This ingenious forerunner of all modern fitted kitchens, designed for Ernst May's New Frankfurt social housing project, had a significant impact on affordable housing, and its embedded logic has been the DNA of all domestic kitchens ever since. Quite surprising, considering how specifically it was originally tailored to the life of the typical household of its time: a large extended family with a full-time housewife and shared daily meals at set times. So, in our research-based design project, we asked what it would mean to adjust the spatial typology of this domestic kitchen according to the demographic shifts, environmental concerns and technological developments of our times.

Margarete Schütte-Lihotzky,
Frankfurt kitchen,
1926

The architectural logic of the domestic kitchen has not changed much over the last century.

As a result, we proposed the typology of the 'food palace' as a 21st-century semi-public, semi-commercial urban entity. The kitchen is a key element in the city, at a crucial intersection between housing, the urban food supply chain, the mains services and the waste management system. Reconfiguring it can drastically affect our cities' environmental footprint as well as their affordable housing development. At the RA we presented this as a large-scale urban vision, sparking several exciting debates with experts and the general public. But to further develop our ideas we also used this attention to initiate a number of prototype experiments. By the time our RA exhibition ended, we were working on three projects with

developers, community groups and municipalities. In Dublin we advised a co-living development (Inn-stead, 2016), in London we were planning a community kitchen installation (HobHub, 2016), and in Denmark we began to co-organise EASA 2017, Europe's largest international summer school for architecture students, under the theme of 'Hospitality – Finding the Framework'. Here we designed a zero-waste collaborative kitchen and cooking system to feed 600 students a day. We collected food donations to minimise our food expenses, and spent the savings on establishing a permanent community kitchen, Babettes Fredericia Food Lab, for the host town.

Atelier Kite,
HobHub,
London,
2016

In the HobHub project, the kitchen combines a physical and a virtual platform, allowing for convenient shared use and collaborative consumption.

The kitchen is a key element in the city, at a crucial intersection between housing, the urban food supply chain, the mains services and the waste management system.

Atelier Kite,
Babettes Fredericia Food Lab,
Fredericia,
Denmark,
2017

right: The new community food space under construction. Collecting a range of in-kind donations and contributions from local people and businesses created a sense of shared ownership from the start.

opposite: A public town feast marked the transfer of the new community kitchen from its initial use as part of a summer festival to its long-term users in the local community.

Atelier Kite,
Festival Feed,
European Architecture
Students Assembly (EASA),
Fredericia,
Denmark,
2017

A pop-up festival for architecture students became the test site for running a kitchen shared by 600 people. Expenses were minimised by collecting food donations, and the savings used to enable a long-term local community kitchen project, the Babettes Fredericia Food Lab.

Launching an alternative architectural practice is no easy ride. Every day I am painfully aware of my shortcomings, and the inevitable mistakes I make.

Self-Initiation and Research-Based Design in Practice

Essentially, Atelier Kite provides multidisciplinary design, research and consulting services, although we are unlikely to get commissions on that basis. Instead, we pitch tangible project proposals directly to potential clients, thus initiating our own projects. These are based on a range of meaningful challenges that we wish to work on, typically related to affordable housing and urban food systems. Initially, we develop our project ideas much like a tech start-up develops any product. Each must begin with research and demonstration of the relevance of a new idea before we collectively commit to its development with the team. We then gradually seek out possible contexts, clients and collaborators, and ultimately approach them with our version of a pitch deck. Sometimes these specific initial proposals might only serve as a tangible starting point in a conversation, but we hardly get rejected this way. In fact, self-initiation allows us to be unusually selective about our projects.

While the risk we take might appear high, we rarely gamble. Our proposals are rooted in solid research and our offers are quite targeted. We carefully balance elaborate multi-stakeholder projects with simpler private commissions. We are as happy to work with developers as we are easy about projects shifting from our original plans. Our solid commitment and interests inevitably make all projects meander around similar leitmotivs. And as we have gradually been building a distinguishable and consistent profile, one project has started to lead to another with increasing ease. But even so, launching an alternative architectural practice is no easy ride. Every day I am painfully aware of my shortcomings, and the inevitable mistakes I make. I know that much of our efforts will not reach their intended goals, or might ultimately not make a significant difference. Nevertheless, nothing has ever taught me as much as the crazy venture of establishing Atelier Kite, and nothing has ever felt more like making a meaningful contribution to the profession, and thereby the kind of society and future I would like to live in. And that is quite a luxury. ⧈

Text © 2018 John Wiley & Sons Ltd. Images: pp 62–4, 65(r) © Atelier Kite/atelierkite.com; p 65(l) © ullstein bild/Getty Images; p 66(t) © Florian Siegel; p 66(b), 67 © Aleksandra Kononchenko

The Fre of Aest

Adam Nathaniel Furman,
Proposal for a Democratic
Monument,
2017

A proposal for a new kind of town hall that serves
as a vast receptacle both political and symbolic,
with its primary facade acting as a visual debating
chamber for all the aesthetic and decorative
capabilities and outputs of its region. Through
this framework, it encourages new forms of
architectural aesthetics to evolve in each location.

Adam Nathaniel Furman

edom netics

Architecture begins when 'building' ends. This may make it sound like an unnecessary add-on to construction, but – argues London-based designer, educator and writer **Adam Nathaniel Furman** – the architect's function as a spatialiser of aesthetics and meaning is precisely what makes the profession crucially enriching to human existence. Observing how it is too often dominated by a consensus on style and approach that prevents it from embodying the full complexity of its time, he highlights brief past periods of greater aesthetic freedom, and invites today's architects to a similarly open attitude, to create works that are truly inspired – and inspiring.

Architecture is not a child of material necessity, and architects are not really 'needed' in any practical sense. For most of history, in almost every culture, the very notion of 'the architect' has not existed; there were simply builders, who built buildings of greater or lesser importance for clients of greater or lesser importance. Every aspect of building and city-making can occur perfectly well without the architect, except for the one thing which elevates it above being the mere accumulation of material orchestrated in a more or less salutary and efficient manner, and that is aesthetics.

The Fundamental Superfluous

It is difficult to argue in purely economic or practical terms that the aesthetic qualities of building are strictly necessary, because in those terms they are not. It is the same conundrum as Art, a seemingly superfluous commodity apparently super-added to society in a grand act of wasteful expenditure. And yet we cannot do without it. We have never been able to do without it. Without it we are left profoundly ill at ease in environments stripped of visual sustenance and cultural resonance.

That which has been labelled as wilful, unnecessary, impractical and excessive in the Modern age is in fact the most fundamentally human, and most psychologically necessary aspect of the manner in which we transform the world around us. It is the manner in which we bind our physical creations to the intangible and complex world of our mental processes and social interactions. Termites build great engineering marvels, as do spiders and some birds, all of whose constructions fulfil their various purposes with expert and sometimes spectacular aplomb. But it is only we who instinctively prioritise the symbolic, the ritual and the meaningful over the expedient and the efficient. It is only humans that intuitively convert their social relations, internal states, emotions and shared fictions into concrete externalised forms, spaces and visual systems.

From the moment the first groupings of *Homo sapiens* and early societies arose, we find wall paintings and jewellery and bizarre building forms, and a profusion of objects whose existence can be explained only in terms of the symbolic, the spiritual or (to use the reductive contemporary term) the 'decorative'. Through these aesthetic constructs we instinctively craft second natures around ourselves: new, comprehensively manmade environments and spaces that satisfy our inherent desire for a comprehensible order, one that mirrors our internal state, and the shared state of the community in which we find ourselves.

Our epoch, our societies, our localities, the tensions and antinomies and fascinations of the moment, are reified, embodied, abstracted and made physical in a uniquely fulsome manner by architects as both the external environment in which meaningful and mundane events take place, and as the spaces which record and represent the very context of their passing. Architecture invariably compresses the richness of a cultural moment into eloquent material artefacts which speak to the wider culture that created them, and it does this because its great power, its great anthropological niche, its potency and its USP, lie precisely in the apparent aesthetics of functional superfluity, which are in fact anything but superfluous: they are the expressive imperative of a uniquely modern ethnological disposition.

The Expressive Imperative

The incredible, almost biological imperative for us as humans to construct externalised environments of aesthetic meaning and relevance that echo our social and spiritual (or let us say intangible) worlds, is perhaps now more potent, potentially riveting, and yet strikingly out of balance amongst architectural practitioners than it ever has been. If, as I do, one locates the core of the architect's practice as being the constant construction of spatialised aesthetics, embodiments of a given moment of time in material form – everything that begins when 'building' ends – then considering we are in possibly the most dynamic, problematic, complex and technologically sophisticated period in human history, our architecture, and its architects, are doing an impressively good job at not representing it, relating to it or embodying it at all.

In the early 20th century, a host of radical new artists, writers, architects and musicians strove to respond to the massive upheavals of Modernity and urbanisation, and the brave new world of mechanisation, by tearing apart the old terminologies and accepted norms of their respective disciplines, and fashioning entirely novel modes of formal expression. They dug deep to extract the materials with which to fashion the writhing and strange core of what was happening to the world around them at the time as books, poems, shocking new sounds and impossibly eccentric new forms of architecture – even if only on paper at the beginning. Buildings became fragmented cruise liners, dazzling Cubist concoctions and crystal mountains, or vast cantilevering bridges to nowhere, skyscraper fantasy factories and clouds of floating geometric coloured planes. Mies van der Rohe's Friedrichstrasse Skyscraper Project for Berlin (1921) dissolved the massive heft of traditional masonry office buildings into a translucent faceted waterfall of glass, while El Lissitzky's '*Wolkenbügel*' ('cloud-iron') for Moscow (1925) proposed huge floating highrises frozen above the city in permanent, dynamically static flight; and in Italy between 1912 and 1914 Antonio Sant'Elia envisioned a visionary 'Città Nuova' (New City) in which buildings became expressive machines of Modernity, that crashed together infrastructure, industry, inhabitation and art into dazzlingly evocative vignettes. For the first time Architecture vigorously took up – with revolutionary and diverse results that resonate to this day – the challenge of creating new aesthetic systems that captured and froze the richness of the fleeting, modern present.

The challenge laid down by Charles Baudelaire in his 1863 essay 'The Painter of Modern Life'[1] – in which he focuses the eye not on the timeless or the traditionally beautiful, but on the new forms of life, and the harsh, arrhythmic, electricity-lit bustle of the newly teeming capitalist metropolis, calling for it to be celebrated and captured by art – was finally and brilliantly answered by the profusion of new architectural forms of expression that emerged forty years later, at the beginning of the 20th century.

Until this point, architecture had mostly embodied static systems and embedded hierarchies; but as capitalism, democracy and industrialisation refashioned the West into a machine of ceaseless change, in which hierarchies and systems were constantly forced into states of radical crisis and flux, the aggressive churn, the constant productive instability of the contemporary city came to demand expression, and became simply untenable without it. Without its own iconographical mythology, without its own concrete, tangible visual manifestations that gave it body and shape, the extreme instability, precariousness and abstraction of the forces at play in the contemporary economy were left terrifyingly incomprehensible, unbearably omnipresent and yet totally impalpable.

The more complex and dynamic our environment becomes, the more we need to see its various conflicting facets frozen, captured and conveyed, which is what happened again for a period from the 1960s. Society and the nature of work, production and consumption was once again being convulsed by change, and once again architects answered Baudelaire's challenge, unleashing a nebula of responses to the contemporary condition, generating a new ecosystem of architectural aesthetics that critiqued and embodied a period of jet travel, space exploration, corporate computers, consumer society, the commodification of history, youth rebellion and the emergence of popular culture, amongst much else besides. In Italy Superstudio were proposing a manmade world of technology that would free us of objects, set against geological-scale structures – the continuous monument (1969) – of pure geometry, that would march around the globe in harmony with, rather than aggression towards, the natural environment. In Austria Hans Hollein was mooring aircraft carriers like huge ancient monuments in wheat fields (1964), and his Retti candle store in Vienna (1966) was a tiny, inscrutable space-age relic of eerily potent symbolic power, while in America Charles Moore was developing an architecture centred on the body and the imagination with his own house in New Haven (1966), and Robert Venturi was exploring design as a complex communicative language, most famously with his Vanna Venturi House in Philadelphia (1964).

Both of these eras of exceptional aesthetic production and creativity were marked by the absence of any consensus or uniformity. They were characterised instead by the emergence of a plethora of highly defined and exceptionally well-articulated competing aesthetic positions, unified only by a shared interest in the nature of the present, in all its profuse difficulty. It is in these moments – for the reasons previously mentioned – of apparently terrifying change, that the pursuit of new aesthetics tends to rise with particular potency to the fore, becoming needed, sought after and much discussed; and this has to happen, can only happen, in something of a vacuum.

Hans Hollein,
Retti candle shop,
Vienna,
1966

Searching for architectural compositions that were simultaneously space-age, futuristic, and yet ancient, resonant and mystical, even in the tiniest of works, Hollein managed to capture the paradoxical impulses of highly technological society longing for the ancient and the atavistic.

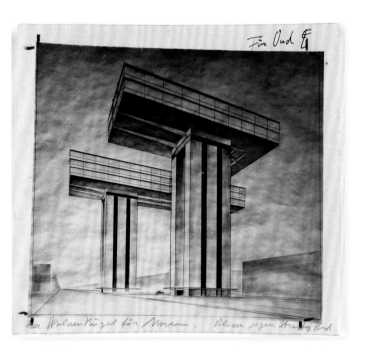

El Lissitzky,
The 'Wolkenbügel': view towards Strastnoj Boulevard,
Moscow,
1925

One of the early 20th century's many radical artist-architects, El Lissitzky proposed these vast, cantilevered offices called Wolkenbügel ('cloud-irons') freed from Earth's gravity by human prowess, and reaching towards completely new architectural forms of expression that could only make sense in the turmoil of a fast-changing industrial and political environment.

Charles Moore,
Bed in the Charles Moore House,
New Haven, Connecticut,
1966

Incorporating motifs, techniques and strategies from popular culture, architectural history and fine art, as well as refocusing space on the individual and his or her bodily senses, Charles Moore created interiors and architecture that were as radical in their contemporary relevance as was the Pop art, or Hippie culture, of the time.

The Tyranny of the Collective

In a lecture at Oxford University in 1958, the liberal philosopher Isaiah Berlin described the concept of 'negative liberty', the freedom from interference and external constraint on individual activity, as being a vital gauge on Modernity's ever-present threat of creeping totalitarianism.[2] Rather than emphasising the creation of enabling frameworks that might unwittingly – and, worse, knowingly – encourage specific outcomes, he stressed that absence, the vacuum of pure autonomy, was the only certain way of ensuring liberty as he saw it on the one hand, and a true plurality of outcomes on the other.

There is a tendency in architecture towards the vilification of precisely these febrile and brilliant periods of exploration and engagement with the present. They are seen as moments of disorder and entropy, perhaps at best suffered because out of them is expected to emerge a new, comprehensibly uniform order. Histories of architecture prefer to smooth over the irreconcilable pluralities of these moments with impossibly restrictive terms like Modernism and Post-Modernism, that categorise the vigour of competing individualities and groupings within necessarily limited definitions which neuter their discreteness, withdraw their venom and kill their spirit, like a menagerie of drugged, sad, soporific animals from all over the planet on display in a cage generically labelled 'jungle'.

There is an irrepressible human desire for unity, for common languages and shared beliefs amongst architects, a fear of chaos. We can see this now as critics decry the 'crisis' in architecture, the lack of an architectural language that has a specifically agreed set of meanings, the longing for the days of Modernism after it closed in on itself and became uniform and unchanging. It has always been this way, and this – as Berlin would have pointed out – is evidence of the perpetual pull towards totalitarianism, a terror of the contemporary world and all its inherent plurality manifest as the nostalgic drive towards unity.

At its heart is a fundamental unease with Modernity, and the complexity and diversity it is wont to bring about. Architects of this disposition may often deploy the formal tropes of a Modernist architectural language, but its use belies a profoundly anti-Modern attitude that has much more in common with the conservative ethos that yearns for a similar unity and stasis, but dresses itself up, more honestly, in classical or traditional garb. Those who seek unity and conformity will naturally see those who do not conform to their notion of acceptable pursuits as being threatening to their understanding of the world, because to a personality of this kind, the potential validity of an alternative approach would invalidate their universal system, and so they will act accordingly to neutralise the threat.

The sphere of architectural discourse, in a kind of reverse entropy, tends to congeal in this direction, with a critical environment that acts much to reinforce an extremely narrow set of accepted aesthetic approaches, and to actively exclude all others through either ridicule or omission. As a result, architects are encouraged through lifelong conditioning to operate within set parameters, failing which they risk disappearing or being condemned. In such times there is in effect no 'negative liberty' for practitioners – rarely a freedom 'from', only inducements 'to'. These periods of consensus are however inherently unstable, brittle, and unable to adapt to extreme change. Whenever the external circumstances of society move forward to such a degree that the disparity between the profession's cyclopean myopia and the wider new environment are so extreme as to render its aesthetics positively comical in its plainly geriatric decrepitude, the despotic system shatters, and a brilliant new void opens up, a pregnant vacuum into which can rush a thousand new ideas that respond in a thousand novel ways to the emerging, unexplored world outside.

The liberal position is precisely the opposite in that it sees those periods of architectural and aesthetic fecundity as something not to be suffered, but actively fostered and – ideally – constantly fought for. It is not a relativistic free-for-all in which everything is equally valuable and so nothing is any longer of any distinct worth, but rather a pluralistic parliament of competing interests and ideas which are in perennial, but respectful, conflict – a vigorous and perpetually fruitful exchange of profoundly held beliefs and carefully worked-out methodologies, whose only truly shared value is to ensure that no one group or cluster of interests come to dominate and impose any kind of orthodoxy on the rest. Much in the way that our liberal democracies have institutionalised a minimal degree of plurality, division and difference at every given moment in time, so a profession which at its very best is an embodiment of the society which it is constantly helping to house, should endeavour to be equally plural at all times.

Those who seek unity and conformity will naturally see those who do not conform to their notion of acceptable pursuits as being threatening to their understanding of the world

Shin Takamatsu,
Pharaoh Dental Clinic,
Kyoto,
Japan,
1984

During the 'bubble' years of Japan's great economic boom, unprecedented architectural forms developed that united references from across the country's cultural spheres, expressing in built form the simultaneously giddy and excited, dystopian, wealthy and apocalyptic mood that was gripping the nation.

内橋小児歯科クリニック

The Terrible Beauty of the Contemporary

We are rapidly moving into the early phases of another great period of change, the effects of which are plain to see all around us, of digital, biological and technological revolution, economic turmoil, media transformation, convulsive political ferment, the simultaneous collapse and apotheosis of globalisation, and the re-evaluation of the very ground of our subjectivity as human beings. The symbolically brain-dead architecture of our recent mute consensus has passed the point at which it looks ridiculous in the face of this brave new world. Everything has moved light years passed it, so far beyond that its buildings appear like the palaces of poor King Ludwig II of Bavaria who in the late 19th century built vast stage sets for himself where he could live in solitude, imagining a world in which monarchs were still absolute sovereigns.

Our built environment, our architecture, is not engaging with the contemporary in any visual way. It is not tearing up the aesthetic rule book and generating multiple new modes of visual and spatial composition; it is not straining every limb to explore ways in which it can once again do its job and reify, make concrete and tangible, the orgasmic horror of the contemporary situation. It has stuck its head firmly in the sand and is dreaming of simpler times long past, of factories and self-built wooden cottages and village communities, the brick warehouses of Empire, and at best the glory days of early Modernity and 'Post-Modernism'. Acre upon acre of our cities are being stuffed with brick and concrete gridded buildings that seem to compete for how little they say, or do, or stand out.

Our built environment, our architecture, is not engaging with the contemporary in any visual way.

It is well and truly time for us to be open to the self-evident fact that architecture is primarily an aesthetic discipline, and that seen in this light it is even more of a weighty and meaningful pursuit: one full of gravitas, social and cultural significance, and portent. It is a discipline whose output can embody, materialise and preserve the complexities of the voluble present – and what a present we are living through now – but it can only do this if it allows for a plurality of voices, of approaches; that is, if it constantly strives to be a territory of aesthetic liberty.

The current version of these repeat architectural consensuses is coming to an end. A vacuum is coming, and we must hope that what may emerge to fill it will be a new, protean and many-faced fascination with the present in all its pulsating incarnations – a plethora of new aesthetic systems and forms for architecture that will make full use, and wield the complete power of, the freedom that can be found in aesthetics. ⌂

Notes
1. Charles Baudelaire, *The Painter of Modern Life*, Penguin (London, New York and Toronto), 2010 (first published in French in 1863).
2. Isaiah Berlin, 'Two Concepts of Liberty', in *Four Essays on Liberty*, Oxford University Press (Oxford), 1969.

Freddy Mamani Silvestre,
'Cholet' events space,
El Alto,
Bolivia,
2015

opposite: An entirely new architectural language has recently been evolved in Bolivia, which fuses international references and local Aymara culture.

below: The new 'Andean' architectural aesthetics express the community's growing wealth, its trade connections with China and its cultural and ornamental traditions, amongst other references.

Embassy Gardens Phase II,
London,
2017

A whole new district of London being built in complete accordance with the current architectural consensus.

Freedom Via Soft Order

Patrik Schumacher

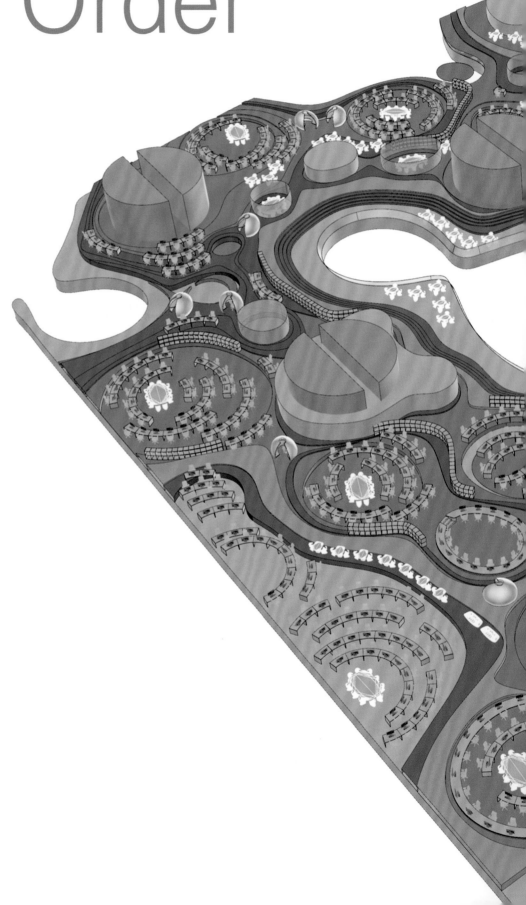

Zaha Hadid Architects,
Sberbank Technopark,
Skolkovo Innovation Centre,
Moscow,
due for completion in 2019

The life process of a firm is ordered via a rich typology of communicative situations defined by the designed settings/spaces that premise and prime the communicative interactions which are expected to take place within them. Design: Christos Passas with Zaha Hadid and Patrik Schumacher.

Architecture as a Foil for Social Self-organisation

Various radical thinkers have categorised architectural ordering as 'violence' and architecture as 'prison'. But the built environment is an integral part of all human society. Could individual and societal freedom be enhanced by a shift from the 'hard order' of the past to a new, libertarian 'soft order'? **Patrik Schumacher**, principal of Zaha Hadid Architects, examines the theoretical background of the subject and points to such a new order, in which intervisibility is key and physical boundaries are replaced by expressive thresholds that act as guiding orientations rather than tools of exclusion or containment.

Freedom as a theme within architecture starts with the modern movement: the free plan, the free facade, free-flowing space. The theme got another boost via late-1960s counter-culture movements and was expressed in the pursuit of lightness and flexibility via spaceframes, capsules, inflatables, 'instant architecture',[1] play-scapes and the informality of adhocism.[2] The 1960s seemed to promise technological utopias where the city was conceived as a freewheeling play-scape for life beyond scarcity of a posited '*homo ludens*' engaged in playful creative self-transcendence. However, progressive liberation experienced disillusionment, both within architecture and within society at large. It is my contention here that now the expansion of freedom can get a viable new lease of life, both in contemporary society and in its architecture, via libertarianism and parametricism.

Freedom, Foresight, Economy and Society

Freedom is our penultimate value. As living systems we strive to maintain the degrees of freedom we have attained in order to navigate a hostile world. The basic evolutionary beginning of freedom of action is to move out of harm's way. The more moves a creature can make – that is, the more degrees of freedom the creature acquires – the greater are its chances to persist. Freedom is advantageous, and most sentient creatures instinctively resist shackles and controls. Freedom must be coupled with cognition and ideally with foresight. Freedom to act crucially includes freedom to plan and prepare, and indeed to labour, so as to make the environment more hospitable and predictable. This implies the self-binding of actions as part of a planned, goal-oriented concatenation of actions, and requires self-discipline. The freedom to act becomes the freedom to pursue projects. The means for preparing, safeguarding and improving our inherently problematic survival are always scarce. Scarcity and thus economy remain ineradicable aspects of the human condition.

Our ancestors discovered, more by chance rather than by insight, that social cooperation and organisation offer momentous productivity advantages that can make our path through the world much more secure. The formation of ever larger societies with their attendant increase in social cooperation points the way towards greater emancipation from the burdens and threats of the physical world. However, societal organisation also implies rules that constrain freedom. Thus a new battlefront for the striving of freedom has opened up: emancipation from societal strictures. Disputes about what constitutes necessary versus unnecessary, or even oppressive, societal restrictions have become a permanent part of the human condition and of our interminable striving for freedom. Our striving has thus become a complicated double agenda – physical emancipation and social emancipation – whereby the two sub-agendas often appear to conflict. Global sustainable freedom is thus hardly a simple matter.

Mies van der Rohe,
Barcelona Pavilion,
1929

Modernism set architecture free from archetypes via abstraction, implying free composition without the strictures of symmetry and proportion, set walls and envelope free from structural loads (free plan, free facade), and promoted a free-flowing space. Plan redrawn and adapted by Patrik Schumacher.

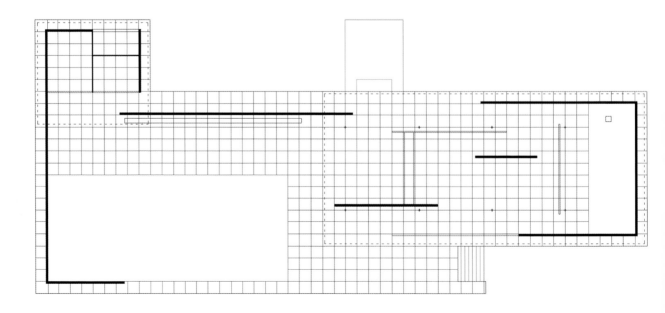

Architecture as Medium of Societal Evolution

The initial formation of human societies was the unique take-off point for an accelerated evolutionary trajectory that has ushered in the Anthropocene and our current global civilisation. Architecture was (and remains) an indispensable factor in establishing this new type of evolution: societal evolution. It is the built environment that provides societal evolution with the cross-generational, material substrate by means of which an advantageous social order can persist and grow. Human settlements form ever larger and more differentiated spatio-material structures, as the skeleton for increasingly complex social structures.

Architecture facilitates social order. The societal function of architecture is the organisation and stabilisation of social cooperation via the territorialising differentiation of activities and persons. This function is a universal necessity of all social formations and includes social control via discriminatory access restrictions as an inevitable feature of any spatialised social order. These restrictions might be posited by a central territorial authority or in a decentralised way by the several landowners in a society based on private property. In the classical liberal conception of society, organised authority was to be based on the rule of law and charged with the protection of life, liberty and property, conceived as natural rights. To hold onto and freely dispose over one's homesteaded or legally acquired property was seen as a fundamental right, and the property itself as an indispensable source of individual autonomy and freedom. The boundary lines that establish property demarcations are at the root of any architectural ontology. The owners have a protected freedom (and thus predictability) within these bounds and are thereby free to limit and regulate the degrees of freedom of all others invited into the territory. In modern societies authority is much more centralised and the rights/freedoms of owners versus non-owners have been redistributed away from owners. In the recent decades of the neo-liberal revolution the pendulum has swung back somewhat.

The question whether overall human emancipation has been enhanced or reduced by these regime shifts remains a controversial issue and depends on one's appraisal of the relative information-processing and decision-making capacity of market processes versus political processes. In my appraisal this depends on historically evolving technological conditions which can at least partially explain these regime shifts as rational adaptations. This appraisal is considering the unprecedented variation and innovation potentials opened up by the digital revolution and the markets' parallel processing

capacity. Privatisation might expand further and market processes might eventually substitute all political decision processes. The unleashing of further freedom in the form of entrepreneurial creativity would allow for the utilisation of the market process as a fertile discovery process in this new environment ripe with innovation potential. There is no reason to expect that further privatisation – including that of all urban spaces – will lead to a situation where parts of society remain excluded or not catered for. What can emerge instead under a new regime – the regime of libertarian anarcho-capitalism – is a versatile and continuously differentiated urban texture weaving synergies across multiple overlapping publics catered for by private providers. Parametricism delivers the congenial architectural translation of the synergetic programmatic organisation discovered and optimised via profit-and-loss signals within the market process.

The Revolt Against Architecture

Even in a society without private property, territorial demarcations will be a necessary social ordering substrate via activity allocations with respectively restricted access and degrees of freedom. Architecture and freedom (just like society and freedom) are thus always already in tension. That is why radical nonconformists like the French intellectual and literary figure Georges Bataille see architecture as prison, as the enemy. Writing in 1929, Bataille argued: 'Architecture is the expression of the very being of societies, ... that which orders and prohibits with authority, expresses itself in what are architectural compositions. ... Moreover, the human order is bound up from the start with the architectural order.'[3]

Architecture facilitates social order. The societal function of architecture is the organisation and stabilisation of social cooperation via the territorialising differentiation of activities and persons.

The radical left-wing architectural blogger and polemicist Léopold Lambert is building on Bataille's anti-architecture and anti-establishment approach: 'The line is architecture's representative medium; it creates diagrams of power that use architecture's intrinsic violence on the bodies to organise them in space.'[4] Architecture is identified with the physical operation of the wall as means of control and exclusion: 'Each wall creates social conditions on both of its sides: the included and the excluded.'[5] As with Bataille, the prison becomes the paradigm case for architecture's social mode of operation: 'There is a violence inherent to architecture, which is then necessarily instrumentalised politically.'[6] Lambert refers to gates, doors and keys as instruments that establish who can get past architecture's violence and who cannot. It is these 'violent' architectural devices that, according to Lambert, can transform a regular house into a prison cell.

If civilisation depends on architectural ordering, it cannot all be summarily dismissed. Therefore we must introduce the distinction between good and bad ordering, good and bad 'violence'. Lambert can avoid this because all the examples and topics he engages with in his blog are exceptional situations like (suppression of) protests, oppressive exclusion of marginal groups, war, occupation (as in Gaza) etc, where, especially from a left-wing perspective, good versus bad, friend versus enemy in terms of oppressed and oppressor, can be taken for granted without being problematised. So here all architectural 'violence' seems obviously bad and is indeed often associated with real violence in the ordinary sense of the word. But on this basis a general theory of the emancipatory or oppressive effects of forms of architectural order cannot be forthcoming.

Robin Evans's 'Towards Anarchitecture' (1970) is to my knowledge the only text that makes freedom explicitly its central topic.[7] Anarchitecture for Evans means something like non-architecture; he also talks about 'the tectonics of non-control' and the 'need to clarify the relationship between "architecture" and human freedom'.[8] His discourse starts with the observation that the physical world offers variable resistance to our freedom of action. He calls this the 'resistance of the ambient universe' and emphasises that the introduction of new physical systems gives rise to novel action types.

Evans presumes designers to be 'committed to providing maximum "choice" or maximum "freedom"'.[9] He focuses his attention primarily on technical systems' transformative impact, and emphasises architecture's physical (rather than 'symbolic') operations. Just as for Georges Bataille and Léopold Lambert, here too the prison serves as an archetype illustrating architecture's essential modus operandi. Evans distinguishes positive, freedom-enhancing interferences from negative interferences restricting freedom. As an example of 'positive interference' he cites the telephone network 'allowing certain novel actions without disallowing any others'.[10] He contrasts this with the prison as a negative example: 'The walls of the prison are there for the sole purpose of frustrating certain kinds of action. …Their function is to narrow down the scope of action of a given set of persons.'[11]

As will be further elaborated below, this narrow conception of architectural operations as physically restrictive is leading us astray. The revolt against architecture in the name of freedom is thus misconceived.

I am more sympathetic when Evans takes a stance against planners and architects 'as arbiters of other people's patterns of life' and is trying to contrast imposing order on living/social systems with imposing order on technical systems, distinguishing 'software order' and 'hardware order' and suggesting that the latter could be substituted for the former, as it were: running a freewheeling human software on a systematically ordered hardware. Evans is not elaborating this point any further than hinting that the power of hardwired computer networks could promise an answer that leaves human users unshackled.

I would like to pick up his suggestive distinction and idea of a systematic order of things that substitutes for the strict prison-like shackling and channelling of human bodies to achieve social order. Evans's idea is reminiscent of Friedrich Engels's inspiring dictum that (under communism) 'the government of persons is replaced by the administration of things'.[12] However, in contrast to Robin Evans, I believe that architecture can deliver towards this promise of emancipation and does not have to hand the baton to digital technology.

I believe that architecture can deliver towards this promise of emancipation and does not have to hand the baton to digital technology.

Architecture as Substrate for Self-organisation

No doubt, we are bodies and architecture sometimes physically orders/channels us. But that is only one aspect of architecture's social functioning: it also functions as an ordering matrix for self-directed browsing and self-sorting. And more importantly, it operates also via thresholds and demarcation lines that do not constitute physical barriers at all, but rather function like signals, indications and indeed communications. Here architecture orders via its information-richness and communicative capacity rather than channelling bodies as the prison paradigm suggests. Thus the 'hard' architectural ontology of walls, fences, locked gates etc should be de-emphasised and replaced by a 'soft' ontology of expressive thresholds, indications and atmospheres that operate semiologically as guiding orientations, invitations and priming characterisations, in short as language rather than as physically operating apparatus of exclusion.

Users set free to roam across an intricately ordered matrix of distinctions – for instance in a continuous office landscape like Frank Gehry's new Facebook campus in Silicon Valley (2015) – might be seen as a compelling instantiation of Engels's dictum quoted above. To speak of architectural 'violence' in this context lacks all plausibility. As violence proper recedes and altogether disappears in the advanced arenas of world society, so does the predominance of physical barriers as spatial ordering mechanisms. Their gradual disappearance from architecture and their substitution by informational architectural operations is a clear sign of societal progress and constitutes a compelling productivity-boosting advantage for those institutions that push forward along this trajectory. The simultaneity of inter-aware offerings, the light-footedness of switching between activity and interaction modes, the overall intricacy and dynamism

Frank Gehry,
Facebook Headquarters,
Menlo Park,
Silicon Valley,
California,
2015

The scheme accommodates 2,800 engineers in a single warehouse-like room that distributes, frames, stabilises and coordinates the collaborative process within a spatial matrix that allows the users to self-sort as participants of various specific social interactions.

of the cooperative process that motivates the co-location in the first place are all striking advantages of an informational spatial order – which we might term 'soft order' – over its physically segregating nemesis 'hard order'. There is no space here to elaborate further on this concept of an informationally operating, empowering and emancipating architectural order. However, the author has elaborated this theme elsewhere, both with respect to the urban scale and with respect to the architectural and interior scales. Regarding the latter, a prior ⌀ article entitled 'Advancing Social Functionality Via Agent-Based Parametric Semiology' discusses communicative architectural ordering for free agents, especially in relation to activity-based corporate space planning in the context of increasingly self-directed patterns of work and collaboration.[13] Regarding the former, another prior ⌀ article, 'Hegemonic Parametricism Delivers a Market-Based Urban Order', elaborates how the techniques and values of parametricism can serve to articulate and empower the programmatic order and synergy potentials of market-allocated urban co-locations-cum-cooperations.[14] The expectation here is that entrepreneurial freedom, guided by market feedback, is the best premise for delivering sustainable, substantive freedom for all urbanites. To deliver this, architecture must ensure that soft order, built on individual freedom, replaces yesteryear's hard order.

Zaha Hadid Architects,
Sberbank Technopark,
Skolkovo
Innovation Centre,
Moscow,
due for completion
in 2019

The life process of a firm is
ordered via a rich typology
of communicative situations
defined by the designed settings/
spaces that premise and prime
the communicative interactions
which are expected to take
place within them. Design:
Christos Passas with Zaha Hadid
and Patrik Schumacher.

Emanuele Mozzo,
Robocrete public
playscape for courtyard
at Università degli
Studi di Milano,
Diploma project,
Studio Hadid/Schumacher,
University of Applied Arts,
Vienna,
2014

above and right: Example of soft order:
here spatial differentiations operate as
suggestive communications, inviting
participants' aleatory appropriation of
the vaguely defined spaces.

There is yet another potential feature – beyond informational guidance – that I would like to include in my concept of 'soft order' put forward here, namely the strategic incorporation of vagueness and indeterminacy – that is, the pursuit of virtuality or 'the virtual'.[15] This concept too resides within the orbit of the semiological project: it implies the withdrawal of information, or semiological de-coding rather than encoding. However, this withdrawal of determinate meaning is best achieved not by emptying the space but by filling it with an abundance of unfamiliar, abstract articulations, as so many invitations for creative appropriation by users.

The essential advantage of a soft architectural order, whether determinate or indeterminate, is that it builds on the freedom of self-directed individuals. A second major advantage is that the absence of physical separations via walls allows for an unprecedented density of simultaneous, intervisible communicative offerings. This makes the construction of a new kind of space possible: the space of simultaneity. To maximally exploit this possibility of total interawareness, I am promoting the idea of the mega-atrium or hollow building where an internal navigation void replaces the usual solid core that blocks all visual communication. Freedom and awareness of opportunities must increase hand in hand. ⌀

Notes
1. A slogan of the British 1960s group and magazine 'Archigram'.
2. Adhocism is the self-explanatory name Charles Jencks gave to a 1960s architectural tendency identified by him in 1972: Charles Jencks and Nathan Silver, *Adhocism: The Case for Improvisation*, 1972, reprint MIT Press (Cambridge, MA), 2013.
3. Georges Bataille, *Architecture* (1929), in *Oeuvres Complètes* (12 vols), Gallimard (Paris), 1971–88, vol 1, pp 171–2.
4. Léopold Lambert, *The Funambulist Papers: Volume 1*, Punctum Books (New York), 2013, p 6.
5. 'Who Welcomes this Violence?', Léopold Lambert in conversation with C, recorded 2 April 2015, http://www.c-o-l-o-n.com/3_1lambert.html.
6. *Ibid.*
7. The author was pointed towards Robin Evans's early and obscure but important contribution via a recent lecture: Lei Zheng, 'Architecture Beyond Form', lecture given at the AA LAWuN (Locally Available World unseenNetworks) symposium, Architectural Association School of Architecture, London, 2 November 2016.
8. Robin Evans, 'Towards Anarchitecture', *Architectural Association Quarterly*, January 1970, reprinted in: Robin Evans, *Translations from Drawing to Building and other Essays*, Architectural Association (London), p 12.
9. *Ibid*, p 13.
10. *Ibid*, p 14.
11. *Ibid*.
12. Friedrich Engels, *Socialism: Utopian and Scientific*, Simplicissimus Book Farm, 1901 (original German: *Die Entwicklung des Sozialismus von der Utopie zur Wissenschaft*, 1883).
13. Patrik Schumacher, 'Advancing Social Functionality Via Agent-Based Parametric Semiology', in Patrik Schumacher (ed), ⌀ *Parametricism 2.0: Rethinking Architecture's Agenda for the 21st Century*, March/April (no 2), 2016, pp 108–13.
14. Patrik Schumacher, 'Hegemonic Parametricism Delivers a Market-Based Urban Order', in Patrik Schumacher (ed), ⌀ *Parametricism 2.0: Rethinking Architecture's Agenda for the 21st Century*, March/April (no 2), 2016, pp 114–23.
15. See: John Rajchman, 'The Virtual House', *ANY Magazine*, 19/20, 1997; also: Brian Massumi, 'Sensing the Virtual, Building the Insensible', in Stephen Perrella (ed), ⌀ *Hypersurface Architecture*, 5–6, 1998, pp 16–25.

Zaha Hadid Architects,
Mega-atrium,
Hyundai Headquarters,
Seoul,
2015

Competition proposal. The mega-atrium tower as a space of simultaneity and maximal interawareness is offered here as a new tower typology well adapted to the communicative requirements of post-Fordist network society.

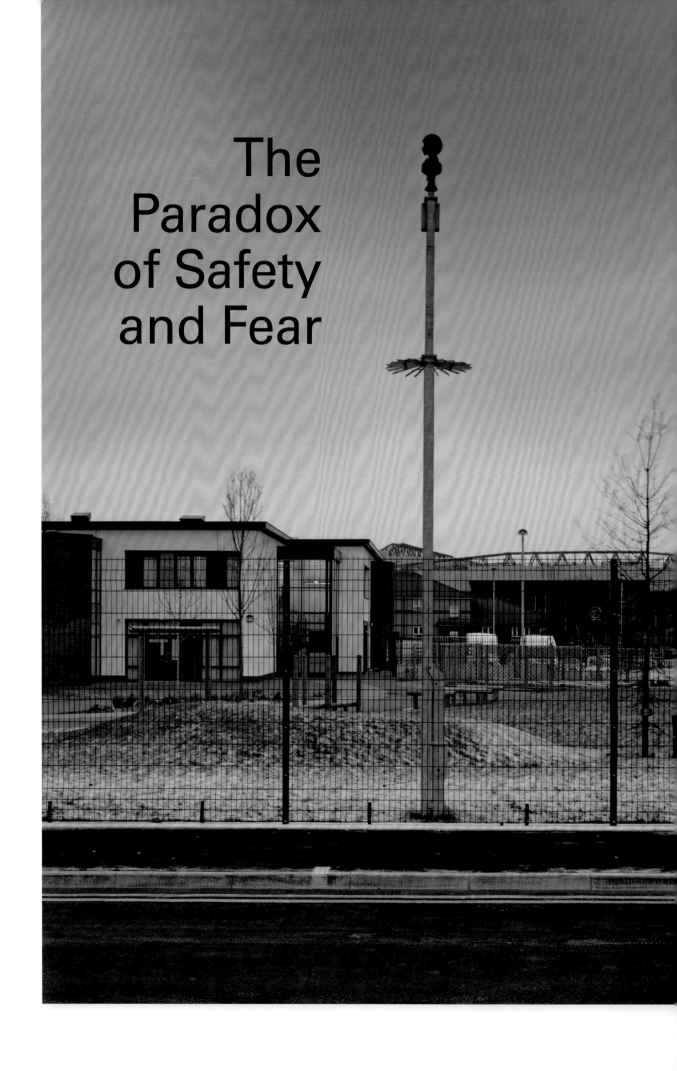

The Paradox of Safety and Fear

Anna Minton

Security
in Public
Space

Security outside Four Oaks Primary School,
Liverpool,
2012

High-security fencing and CCTV loom over this primary school.

Ever-increasing levels of security staff presence and enclosure around public spaces may be counterproductive. Rather than reassuring and liberating us, the phenomenon – prevalent in the UK and the US but far less so in other countries – is arguably creating a heightened sense of fear, and is limiting the expression of our democratic society. **Anna Minton**, a widely published author and speaker who is currently Reader in Architecture at the University of East London, reflects on the plague of public-space privatisation, and points to positive initiatives that are going against the flow.

When one day in 2007 the British Library suddenly introduced security guards and bag searches at its entrance, shocked visitors were told that security had been increased because the Queen was visiting. As an iconic public building, the intrusive security that regular users of the library were told was only temporary seemed to sit oddly with this national symbol of public life and freely available culture, and a decade later the bag searches are still there.

In the intervening years, security has become ubiquitous. From the machine-gunned police and panoply of surveillance equipment that greet visitors to its airports, to the crash barriers disfiguring the Houses of Parliament and the Ring of Steel in the City of London, the capital can seem to be in lockdown, with highly visible security also omnipresent in many of its public buildings and public places, often justified as protection for the public and a necessary response to the ongoing 'War on Terror'. Protection is also often given as the reason for 5-metre (16-foot) high fences and remote-controlled entrances at schools and children's centres.

A similar situation prevails in the US, where universally armed police and gun culture meld with an increasingly high-security environment. What the UK and the US also share in common is a spiralling fear of crime that has no relation to actual crime figures, which in general have been falling for decades. However, in cities across Europe, including those that have been victims of terror attacks, the response is very different. Airport security is far less intrusive, there are no bag checks in Berlin's museums, and very little visible CCTV in Athens and in Copenhagen, while Italy's school buildings have won awards for their openness and transparency. At the same time, fear of crime in Europe is far lower than in Britain and America, leading to the paradoxical conclusion that rather than providing reassurance, security actually increases fear and distrust between people.[1]

While the War on Terror may be the justification provided for the roll-out of high security, the hardening of the built environment, as it is sometimes called, long preceded the 9/11 attacks on the World Trade Center. As far back as 1981, criminologists Clifford Shearing and Philip Stenning put forward their 'mass privatisation thesis', which described the spread of mass private property in the form of shopping malls, finance districts, airports, leisure parks, conference centres, university and hospital campuses, and gated communities.[2] Their insight was that this inevitably brought with it private security, as private property is always policed by private security. In time, this also became tied to insurance premiums, which began to demand private security. While security needs in public places remained tied to the rule of law, with the police focused on crime prevention, on private land the primary concern would be the protection of property and the limiting of access to private estates. What we have now started to see is that the way the privately owned parts are policed by security and surveillance has spread into the public life of the city, as witnessed by the roll-out of private estates which critics describe as 'malls without walls'.

Countryside Homes, Salford, Greater Manchester, 2012

Housing in Salford ringed with fencing of different types and CCTV cameras.

Defensible Space

In fact, almost a decade before the 'mass privatisation thesis' it was becoming clear that political attitudes to crime and design were fast changing, spearheaded by the influence of Oscar Newman, a Canadian architect working in New York. His *Defensible Space: People and Design in the Violent City* (1972)[3] emerged in a climate of growing concern over the rise in crime that appeared to be sweeping urban America, fuelling fears that the US was experiencing a breakdown of society. Investigating the link between crime and the design of the environment in deprived parts of New York, his research took hold on both sides of the Atlantic, leading to a new political and intellectual philosophy for crime and its prevention that expounded the virtues of private space, individual responsibility and territoriality. As such it chimed with the rise of neo-liberalism and moved centre-stage with regard to urban policy in both America and Britain.

Newman's work provided a relatively simple and cost-effective answer, arguing that rather than engaging with complex social problems as the causes of crime, design could offer 'can do' solutions that people could take responsibility for and which, he claimed, worked in even the poorest areas. From his study of the three New York housing schemes, he found that 'territoriality' created space that could defend itself. He took aim at the Modernist design of estates and tower blocks in particular as producing crime (Manhattan tower blocks notwithstanding), and recommended they be knocked down and replaced with low-rise housing where private territory and boundaries could be defended. Clearly marked-out boundaries would give residents a sense of ownership, encouraging them to look after their patch and discouraging strangers and opportunistic criminals from entering, and so creating safe places.

Despite scepticism in academic circles, where Newman's ideas were criticised for their simplistic environmental determinism, his book was so influential that within two years substantial American funding was made available for the study and implementation of his 'defensible space' concepts – which became known as Crime Prevention Through Environmental Design (CPTED) – and he was employed by the US Department for Housing and Urban Development. A few years later he was invited by the BBC to make a documentary for the influential television series *Horizon*, and by the 1980s his ideas were also starting to determine policy in the UK.

Secured by Design

Heavily promoted by geographer Alice Coleman,[4] who became an advisor to Margaret Thatcher, 'defensible space' paved the way for Secured by Design, which is the British version of CPTED. The government-backed policy started life in 1989 and led to police officers being trained as crime prevention design advisors, known as Architectural Liaison Officers, who adhere to set design standards. Although administered by the Association of Chief Police Officers (ACPO), and describing itself as the 'official UK Police flagship initiative combining the principles of designing out crime with physical security',[5] Secured by Design is now an independent private company funded by 480 companies selling security products that meet its standards,[6] which are today a condition of planning permission on all new development in the UK and in particular for housing, schools and public buildings.

Maryland Point, Newham, East London, 2012

This housing development, notable for its multiple security features, won a Secured by Design award.

The consequence is that Newman's emphasis on territory and individual ownership, which does not sit easily with communal public housing, is now reflected in high-security residential estates where gates, grilles and forbidding fences have become the norm. Secured by Design guidelines also state that security must be greater in high crime areas – which correlate with poverty – with the result that deprived parts of Britain are taking on an almost militarised feel that is alienating and intimidating. Maryland Point, for example, a housing development in East London that received a Secured by Design National Award, has small windows, reinforced steel doors with full-size iron gates in front, and an aluminium roof.

It is the same with schools. The Secured by Design guidance document includes 31 specific recommendations for schools ranging from fencing, gates and bollards to roller shutters and grilles, electronic locking systems, metal detectors and, of course, CCTV. In high crime locations, 'anti ram' bollards are recommended to protect entrances. Reflecting the particularly lucrative nature of the security industry, it is also notable that the 31 products listed link directly to the section of the Secured by Design website where the items can be purchased from its members. Illustrating how strong demand for security is in schools, the director of a company producing security fencing said: 'We started off doing things like prisons, airports … high-security environments, and now we're increasingly doing more schools and multi-use games areas [playgrounds].'[7]

Gated development,
Stockport,
Greater Manchester,
2012

Obtrusive gates surround
this housing development
in Stockport.

Evelyn Grace Academy,
Brixton,
London,
2012

High-security fencing surrounds
this secondary school in Brixton.

Occupy protest,
St Paul's Cathedral,
London,
19 October 2011

Occupy had initially aimed to site its protest outside
the headquarters of the London Stock Exchange, in
privately owned Paternoster Square. Following a
court injunction the protesters instead set up camp
on the public land around St Paul's Cathedral.

Privatisation of Public Space

Although Newman's research initially focused on deprived
areas, today Secured by Design influences all public buildings
and public places. This approach sits easily with the growing
privatisation of public places, which has accelerated sharply
since the 'mass privatisation thesis'. During the boom years
that preceded the 2008 financial crisis, and which witnessed a
wave of new construction across the country, it became clear
that that privately owned estates such as the financial districts
at Canary Wharf and Broadgate, built in the image of business
to serve the needs of business during the 1980s in the former
industrial heartlands of East London, had become the template
for all new development in the UK, including public streets and
public places.

To take just one example, Liverpool One, which was built
just before the financial crash, is an enormous open-air mall
that covers 34 streets in the heart of Liverpool, all of which are
privately owned and policed by uniformed private security who
enforce strict rules and regulations on behaviour and access.
It is the same at Cabot Circus in Bristol, at Westfield Stratford
City in London, and countless other 'malls without walls'. In
addition to rollerblading, skateboarding, cycling and even eating
and drinking in some areas, these places also ban photography,
filming and, critically, political protest, which means they are not
democratic spaces. Ironically, even the headquarters of London's
Mayor, the Greater London Authority, is part of a privately
owned estate called More London, with the consequence that
democratically elected Assembly members are stopped from
conducting television interviews outside their own building.

Advocates claim the Georgian squares and terraces that
include some of the most beautiful parts of London were built
on a similar model, by aristocratic landlords who controlled
the 'great estates', such as the Duke of Westminster who
owned large parts of Mayfair and Belgravia, and the Duke of
Bedford who owned Covent Garden. What they do not say is
that during the 18th and early 19th centuries, the great estates
were closed to the general public, surrounded by high fences
and railings and policed by security guards and sentry boxes.
As local government grew in power, paralleled by the increased
democratic representation that came with the widening of the
electoral franchise, large-scale public protests took place against
the gating-off of such large parts of the city. By 1864–5, after
two major parliamentary enquiries, 163 miles (262 kilometres)
of roads were passed over to local authority control, and 140
toll bars were removed.[8]

Since then it has been customary for local authorities to
'adopt' streets and public spaces, to use the official terminology,
meaning that whether or not they actually own them, they
control and run them. This was a hard-won democratic
achievement, however it is now going into reverse, as was clearly
illustrated by the Occupy protest that took place outside St
Paul's Cathedral in 2011. Despite the stunning visual backdrop,
which helped generate headlines, the protestors had no desire
to be outside St Paul's and had wanted to base the protest
just behind the cathedral, in Paternoster Square, which is the
headquarters of the London Stock Exchange. But Paternoster
Square is privately owned and does not permit protest. It then
emerged that the entire square mile of the City of London is now
a series of privately owned estates, with the exception of a small
space outside the Bank of England where protests often gather.

Although the Peabody Trust made great efforts to limit visible security and tone down the gated element on this estate, it nonetheless includes a fenced games area and internal gates.

This public open space in the heart of Brixton is home to a mingling of diverse uses, from the African and Caribbean War Memorial to pavement tables outside the Ritzy cinema, skateboarders and commuters on their way home.

Given the bleak picture, it may seem surprising but small shoots of hope are emerging, although going against the tide requires persistence and tenacity.

Amanda Levete Architects (AL_A),
V&A Exhibition Road Quarter,
London,
2017

The new entrance, courtyard and gallery are designed to allow people to flow into the museum from Exhibition Road.

'Space Probe Alpha' protest,
City Hall,
London,
2016

Green Party Greater London Assembly member Sian Berry speaks to a crowd gathered for a 'mass trespass' of privately owned public space at City Hall. The event, organised by Berry, geographer and 'place hacker' Bradley Garrett and Anna Minton, attracted hundreds of people to hear speakers including Will Self and Mark Thomas.

De-escalating Security

In this climate do architects in the UK have any chance of countering these threats to freedom and democracy in the city? Given the bleak picture, it may seem surprising but small shoots of hope are emerging, although going against the tide requires persistence and tenacity. Architect Claire Bennie, formerly development director at housing association the Peabody Trust, managed to resist the demands of the Secured by Design police liaison officer to create a gated community at Peabody Avenue, the housing scheme in Pimlico she developed in 2012 – although she had to commission a research study to prove that safety would not be compromised. In Brixton, the central square was expanded and redesigned, with no security guards, and with protests of various kinds a regular feature and skateboarding a daily occurrence. And in 2016 at City Hall, 200 people packed into More London's amphitheatre, the 'Scoop', for 'Space Probe Alpha', an event to protest and reclaim the space that attracted the support of artists and writers including Will Self.

Another gratifying recent development has been the Victoria and Albert Museum's decision to remove bag searches and to resist the council's demands to place bollards and 'hostile vehicle mitigation' (crash barriers) outside the building. According to Vernon Rapley, the V&A's security director: 'I'd become quite concerned about the over-escalation of security and how there was no opportunity to take it back down – that might seem a strange thing for a security director and ex-police officer to say.'[9] Rapley and his team studied security in different places and were influenced by the openness of the Rijksmueum and Van Gogh Museum in Amsterdam which they are keen to emulate, especially since Amanda Levete's new courtyard entrance to the museum and underground exhibition hall opened in 2017. 'We have changed greatly. We are meant to be part of the metropolis, we want people to flow into our courtyard,' he said, adding that he hopes that once one institution changes others will follow. Perhaps there is hope for the British Library after all. ∞⁺

Notes
1. See Anna Minton, *Ground Control: Fear and Happiness in the Twenty-First Century City*, Penguin (London), 2009, pp 168–70.
2. Clifford Shearing and Philip Stenning, 'Modern Private Security: Its Growth and Implications', in Michael Tonry and Norval Morris (eds), *Crime and Justice: An Annual Review of Research*, Vol 3, University of Chicago Press (Chicago, IL), 1981, pp 193–245.
3. Oscar Newman, *Defensible Space: People and Design in the Violent City*, Architectural Press (London), 1972.
4. Alice Coleman, *Utopia on Trial: Vision and Reality in Planned Housing*, Hilary Shipman (London), 1985.
5. www.securedbydesign.com.
6. Anna Minton, 'Fortress Britain: High Security, Insecurity and the Challenge of Preventing Harm', New Economics Foundation working paper, 2013: www.annaminton.com/single-post/2016/03/21/New-report-Fortress-Britain.
7. *Ibid*, pp 6–8.
8. Peter J Atkins, 'How the West End was Won: The Struggle to Remove Street Barriers in Victorian London', *Journal of Historical Geography*, 19, 1993, pp 265–77.
9. Telephone interview with the author, 9 September 2017.

Carlo Cappai and Maria Alessandra Segantini

SEEDS OF LEGACY

HYBRID AND FLEXIBLE SPACES

C+S Architects,
Law-Court Offices,
Venice,
Italy,
2013

The building is the entrance
gate of the redesigned former
tobacco factory which will
house the city's law-court
offices. It is a hybrid building
with a commercial future
public space on the ground
floor.

Public space is being eroded all over the world. Given a lack of political will to tackle the issue, might architects play their part in rectifying it? **Carlo Cappai and Maria Alessandra Segantini,** co-directors of C+S Architects, based in Venice and London, believe so. They advocate designing public buildings with a consideration of communal uses beyond those of the main brief. This, coupled with flexibility to endure changing occupation needs, can make them an asset to the community for generations.

An innovative reconsideration of public buildings and their role within cities and communities can provoke different ways of inventing the present and of planting seeds for a better future. From this perspective, structures such as schools can be considered a great political medium.

Schools were benchmarks of new residential developments in the early 20th century, playing the significant role of secular parallels to churches, as in Willem Marinus Dudok's Geraniumschool (1918), Rembrandtschool (1920) and Bavinckschool (1922) at Hilversum in the Netherlands. Similarly, the open-air school in Amsterdam (1930) by Jan Duiker and Bernard Bijvoet, the one in Suresnes, France (1935) by Eugène Beaudouin and Marcel Lods, and the Karl Marx School in Villejuif, Paris (1933) by André Lurçat – whose form followed new pedagogical principles – became political tools to represent a new democratic world, with open areas and glazed facades turned into symbols of new hygienic spaces where everybody was welcome.

In the expanding suburbs of the postwar period, schools consolidated their role as local public spaces, as famously modelled by the Prestolee Primary School in Manchester, UK under the progressive leadership of Francis O'Neil (headmaster 1918–53), or in the teaching approach established in the northern Italian city of Reggio Emilia from 1950 by educational psychologist Loris Malaguzzi. Their methods were child-centred, putting the main emphasis on experimental learning with reference to the environment and external stimuli, with space being a fundamental tool.[1] More recent examples are found in the architecture of Herman Hertzberger, such as the Montessori School in Delft (1966) and the Willemspark School in Amsterdam (1983), where the boundaries between playgrounds and urban public spaces are erased by the removal of fences and barriers.

But what is the role of these small buildings today? To seek an answer to this question, C+S Architects – based in Venice and London – have produced a body of research and design work under the title 'eduCARE', which the practice was invited to exhibit at the 15th Venice Architecture Biennale in 2016 with the installation *Aequilibrium*. It investigates the potential of space in school typologies, which could essentially become generous spaces activated by people and communities, and can be considered a backbone for discussion on the broader topic of the erosion of public space, which confronts people on a daily basis.

A consistent dramatic erosion of the public domain is not only happening in the physical sphere, but through the silent consent of politicians, the diminished role of political responsibility in the transformation of cities and the complacent undoubting position of the profession in questions such as growth and speed. Symptomatic of this are the facts that market economies are pushing the efficient tech industry to brand a new product, smart cities, which are promoted as solutions to the urgency of ecological questions, security concerns, smart mobility, food and water scarcities; and that free open public space is being constantly reduced in new developments in European contexts, in the name of neatness and security. As for the field of architecture, having changed its scope in the past 30 years and moved from the good intentions of serving welfare policies to slowly supporting and feeding the market economy, it is losing its ambition of autonomy and freedom, and so facing an increasingly marginalised role.

Far from any nostalgic rhetoric of a return to the past, C+S are interested in discovering domains in architecture which can keep some distance from uninspired global markets. As the firm's co-directors, we oscillate between research and practice in a discipline positioned on the threshold between the interests of the private client and a presence in shaping cities and landscapes. We consider ourselves expert travellers, developing progressive insights through recognising and embracing the contradictions and complexity of the contemporary, but still remaining zealous guardians of the public good. This attitude probably has much to do with the particular local context where the practice has grown: Venice.

Venice is a city erected on artificial pieces of land. Since the land itself was the first structure to be created and is the most important to maintain, the city's chief architects – titled Proto della Serenissima – had to be at the same time experts in construction, hydraulics and water supply in order to be able to preserve the equilibrium between the lagoon and its inhabitation. It was exactly this search for balance which generated the magical interior and outdoor spaces that constitute Venice: a series of synthetic solutions to tackle complex problems. The *campo* is a public square as well as a water reservoir for the community living around it; and the *salone* is an adaptable empty space for both the private and public life of a merchant. Aspiring to act as a sort of Proto for contemporary times, the C+S team believes that – whether engaged on public or private commissions – one of the powers of the practice's work is to give back a certain amount of generous, free, adaptable, open and beautifully designed public space to communities.

C+S Architects,
Aequilibrium,
Venice Architecture Biennale,
Venice,
Italy,
2016

Aequilibrium is a cantilevered steel structure which symbolises C+S Architects' approach to schools as open nodes of public space in cities and communities, in the practice's search for a different social, economic and ecological balance.

Aequilibrium investigates the potential of space in school typologies, which could essentially become generous spaces activated by people and communities, and can be considered a backbone for discussion on the broader topic of the erosion of public space

Potentials of Space in School Design

Due to their monofunctional character and very specific programmes, safety regulations and compulsory uses, 'public' buildings such as schools, law courts and administration buildings are often less public than those that are privately owned. This commonly creates a misunderstanding about the potentials that could be generated inside them. By refusing to adopt a purely functional approach and working to hybridise their layout and spatial model, public buildings can not only fulfil the requested brief but also become rich opportunities to generate different scopes: a possibility which is crucial in a moment of economic crisis. The hybridisation of spaces can be turned into a long-term economic and human resource for individuals and communities, incorporating new economic concepts that involve time and knowledge and not only GDP.

To enhance school buildings' potential, C+S Architects looked at them also from the point of view of technical innovation. The open-air school in Amsterdam designed by Duiker and Bijvoet, and Hunstanton School in Norfolk (1954) by Peter and Alison Smithson, are only two of a series of examples where architecture and experimentation with innovative technologies became a provocative political tool, proposing different ways of living and educating. When the classroom became a space open to the outside, the need for lighter desks and chairs that could be easily moved to the open air pushed designers to experiment with new materials and forms to inhabit those spaces. From the single chairs designed by Mart Stam (S33, 1926) or Marcel Breuer (Wassily Chair, 1926) using then newly invented tubular steel, to the research of Jean Prouvé who in the 1940s provocatively worked on a model of a whole school building for series production, quick and easy to assemble and disassemble, the history of school furniture follows the paths of building manipulations and experimentation.

What is happening in the contemporary digital and multicultural world of networks? Could schools be reinvented as new hybrid tools shared by the communities around them? Could they be imagined as manifestoes to educate new generations in a more sustainable and economically fair perspective? Could they be reimagined as a network to reduce pollution or fight inequalities?

Considering their compulsory use, and their being part of an existing network where a multicultural experience happens naturally, schools are new powerful hubs within cities. Working to enhance school buildings' potential, C+S Architects have questioned design processes – from the business plan, to design and construction, to the reinvention of codes (projects by C+S have been used to inform the new codes for school buildings in Italy), to the use of cutting-edge technologies, to civic engagement. Like Elzéard Bouffier, the main character in Jean Giono's allegorical tale *The Man Who Planted Trees* (1953), planting an oak forest acorn by acorn,[2] C+S felt that their task was to plant one school after another.

C+S School Manifesto

When C+S Architects' work was selected for an exhibition at the 2017 Milan Triennale, the firm were asked to synthesise the findings of their investigations in a manifesto on the role of schools in cities and communities.

A first point in the resulting manifesto is that C+S consider schools to be open public spaces rather than correlating them to their programme. In the practice's design approach, functional boxes have been turned into porous vessels by questioning the conventional layout of rows of classrooms along a corridor and instead enhancing the use of the public areas outside school hours. C+S reinvented the model of the school, turning it into a hybrid between a school and a civic centre.

Secondly, the practice uses schools to investigate space potentials rather than delivering a product. Condensing the more public activities around a courtyard – the square – and designing the spaces with glazed walls, the aim is to generate a melting pot of possible experiences. Intervisibility is a key word in C+S's work, where children are exposed to multiple activities that can happen in parallel, during and after school hours. In a similar way, transparency between different spaces guarantees security without a need for digital control, instead pushing children to learn to take care of each other and so fighting phenomena like bullying. All of the practice's school projects have some undefined spaces which can be transformed by the community: a courtyard with a soft floor at Ponzano Primary School (2009); oversized corridors in the nursery school in Covolo, Pederobba (2006); and a roof terrace to be turned into a botanical garden or an art space, plus a central space which can become the community children's library or a place for weekend parties, at Chiarano Primary School (2013). All of these perform a specific task within the school programme, but each allows different exploitation of its potentials and interpretations by the community outside school hours.

C+S Architects,
Nursery School,
Covolo,
Pederobba,
Veneto,
Italy,
2006

Colour is a code to allow
the small children to move
independently around the
space. The central piazza
becomes a community centre
during the weekends.

C+S Architects,
The Kite,
Fontaniva,
Veneto,
Italy,
2014

The correct orientation and
thickness of the concrete
walls has obtained planning
permission without the use
of insulation. The school
generates a circular economy
involving resources from the
community.

C+S Architects,
Ponzano Primary School,
Ponzano, Veneto,
Italy,
2009

The layout and transparency of the walls allows
intervisibility from all sides of the building.

The posters which illustrated the story of
Ponzano Primary School's construction to the
children, and which were part of the community-
participation workshop.

Thirdly, C+S engages with communities through very special participation workshops. To quote the major example, putting on a theatre play for Chiarano Primary School, the children together with the architects acted out the process of designing their new school and presented it to their parents. During the design process for Ponzano Primary School, C+S wrote and illustrated a story about the new school's design and organised an after-school club for storytelling on the theme. Architecture was the topic of discussion with communities while designing schools, playing with light and structure. The simplest words were sought to play a game of architecture with the children and the communities around them, involving them in theatre plays not only so that they could participate in the design process but also to share with them the magic of space-making.

In order to involve the community in the process of financing, planning, designing and building, as well as encouraging the reconsideration of policies and codes and engaging with all the potential stakeholders, C+S instituted 'working tables'. These workshops aim to spread the concepts which drive the firm's ecological approach, as most of its schools are testers of reduced energy consumption and so become manifestoes of environmental sustainability. A combination of cutting-edge technologies with the basic principles of vernacular architecture enables the creation of buildings which can function effectively without insulation. The mechanisms for air cooling and ventilation are made into obvious physical objects, to attract the children's attention and develop their awareness of these topics.

Fourthly, as budgets are often limited, C+S's schools are turned into economic models to fight inequality. On the private market, the Kite school complex in Fontaniva (2013) was designed in collaboration with the owner as an adaptable, low-cost structure together with a business plan to circulate human resources, time-sharing and people skills: it has generated a circular economy for education and fun in the area.[3]

A combination of cutting-edge technologies with the basic principles of vernacular architecture enables the creation of buildings which can function effectively without insulation.

Putting on a theatre play for Chiarano Primary School, the children together with the architects acted out the process of designing their new school and presented it to their parents.

C+S Architects, Chiarano Primary School, Chiarano, Veneto, Italy, 2013

The school's layout is designed to avoid any corridors. The central piazza is turned into the children's public library after school hours. A rooftop botanical garden in the form of a suspended lantern reduces the need for artificial lighting.

A theatre play was written
by the architects and acted
by the children of Chiarano
to tell their parents the
story of their future school.

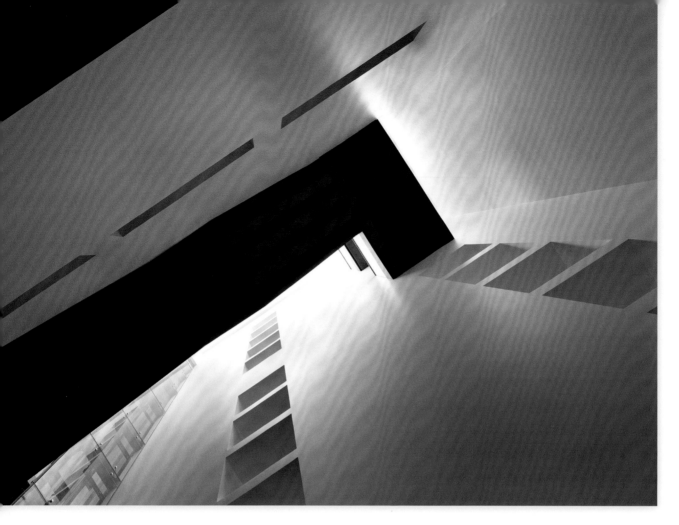

C+S Architects,
Law-Court Offices,
Venice,
Italy,
2013

The interior of the law-court offices is a seven-storey-high top-lit space, recalling typical historic Venetian factories. This 'covered piazza' acts as an entrance space for the former tobacco factory, which has been given back to the citizens after a period in disuse.

C+S Architects,
Water Filtration Plant,
Sant'Erasmo,
Venice,
Italy,
2009

Though programmatically very defined, the building is simply designed with a series of thick walls. The durability of this 1-metre (3-foot) thick structure and the simplicity of its layout will possibly allow different uses in the future.

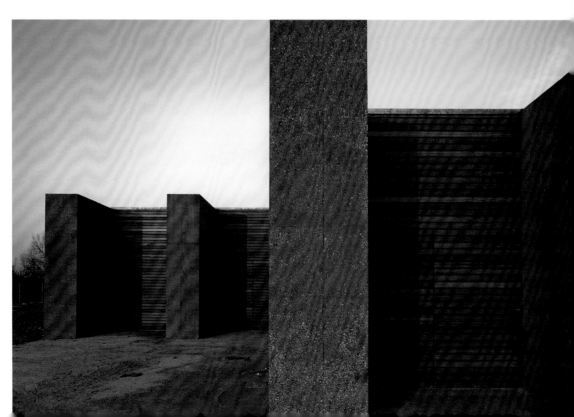

Architecture is a discipline with a memory which is still relevant now and will remain so in the future.

C+S Architects,
The Cord,
Venice Art Biennale,
Venice,
Italy,
2003

The Cord, designed as a commission for the entrance of the 50th Venice Biennale (2003), aimed to force arriving visitors to have the experience of entering a rounded space. The installation was replicated in 15 Italian historic squares to interfere with the conventional setting and activate the public space. One of them was positioned in Venice's Piazza San Marco.

Another key point in the manifesto is that C+S schools are nodes of a network to share resources and fight pollution. The masterplan for the school network of the city of Treviso will allow the municipality to make a series of 'acupuncture' interventions, with the aim of reinforcing the network of public spaces, increasing cycling and pedestrian mobility, and thus reducing pollution and expanding the sense of community around these public open spaces. C+S's strategies have also included the redesign of a series of pedestrian areas and bicycle routes – micro urban interventions to reduce pollution, at the same time as engaging communities to participate in the process. With the introduction of a network of slow-speed lanes, people are able to look after each other, improving security and control through the community rather than building walls or grafting digital technologies. C+S's emphasis on sharing – whether of objects, time or space, from book-sharing to the shared vegetable garden – leads to a new openness of some portions of the school network, which can turn into ethnographic, cooking or sewing labs where people share their skills and resources. The concentration of extracurricular activities reduces children's movement from place to place, fighting pollution and increasing their independence.

Moulding Future Heritage

Architecture is a discipline with a memory which is still relevant now and will remain so in the future. Today, Roman cathedrals are used as retail spaces, and Gothic churches as museums, thanks to the power of potentials implicit in their structures. The focus on spatial potentials is as key to C+S Architects' work in all fields – from law-court offices to infrastructures to housing schemes – as it is in the firm's school projects. This is reflected in the practice's slogan, which summarises an approach to the profession of architecture: 'We mould future heritage, and this is a fundamental freedom and responsibility of our work.' ∆

Notes
1. See Carolyn Pope Edwards, Lella Gandini and George E Forman, *The Hundred Languages of Children: The Reggio Emilia Approach – Advanced Reflections*, Greenwood Publishing Group (Westport, CT), 1998.
2. Jean Giono, *The Man Who Planted Trees*, Harvill Press (London), 1995 (first published in French in 1953).
3. A video of the design concept of The Kite is at https://vimeo.com/82457365

Charles Holland

Wild

Architec

The Potential of Sel

Charles Holland Architects (CHA)
and Invisible Studio,
House in Oosterwold,
Almere,
The Netherlands,
2017

The design exploits the guidelines of the area to propose a tower set in an orchard that is half house and half farm building.

ture

Build settlements

Self-build is all about 'dweller control' – involving people in the creation of their own living environments. **Charles Holland**, a practising architect and Professor of Architecture at the University of Brighton, looks at schemes around the world that manifest different approaches to it: from major projects involving state-commissioned high-profile architects at the initial stage and encouraging subsequent modifications by residents, to others that give inhabitants free rein within certain planning restrictions, to one where architects are out of the picture entirely.

We are familiar with the architectural profession's lament that it has lost power and prestige. Other consultants have taken on roles traditionally associated with architects, and new forms of procurement have handed responsibility to contractors and their project managers. This much we know. But there is a counter-narrative to this story, one that exists on the margins of architecture as a critique of the discipline and of professionalism itself. This narrative regards a desire for authority and prestige as the problem, and sees architecture ultimately as a mechanism of power and control.

The relationship of architecture to power is most obvious in large institutional buildings, governmental projects or infrastructural plans. But it is also subtly present in the domestic realm, in the houses we inhabit and the spaces we call home. Here the ambitions of architects can often be in conflict with the tastes and lifestyles of the residents they are designing for.

What if we turned around architecture's lament, and looked at situations where architects sought out different kinds of roles? What if instead of wanting situations of maximum power and control, architects occupied a more ambiguous role of facilitator, enabler or agent?

The anarchist writer Colin Ward has used the term 'dweller control'[1] to describe situations in which residents become instrumental in how the houses they live in are designed. Sometimes this process is formalised as an explicit part of the brief. In others it arises either through direct action by residents or through the slow process of time and the 'natural' adjustments that happen to houses as they are lived in.

What relation does dweller-control have to these conversations about the role and agency of the architect? Is self-built housing a threat to architects, another nail in the coffin of their marginalisation? Or can it offer a more fundamental realignment of the relationship between residents and the houses they inhabit? In devolving responsibility for some aspects of design, can architects contribute to more responsive and successful housing? And in doing so can they gain influence in other, more strategic areas of spatial planning and development?

What follows is a snapshot of a number of examples where 'dweller control' or the influence of residents has been central to new housing developments. They range across time and geography, from historic examples to current experiments, and demonstrate the creative and inventive capacity of self-build. They include large-scale state-sanctioned projects, cooperative/communal settlements and wild 'off-grid' communities.

Van Eyck's scheme in particular remains a model for the framing of residents' involvement and the possibilities for dweller control

PREVI, Lima

The PREVI (Proyecto Experimental de Vivienda) housing scheme was an experiment in combining top-down planning with resident control, built in Peru in the late 1960s. Working with the United Nations Development Programme, the Peruvian government organised an international architecture competition for a 40-hectare (100-acre) site in Lima. A number of high-profile architects including James Stirling, Charles Correa and Christopher Alexander entered the competition to design around 1,500 housing units. However, instead of picking a single winner, the organisers chose a number of schemes and combined them across the site. The schemes were united, though, by the manner in which they directly encouraged future expansion by the residents.

One of the most interesting and successful was designed by Aldo van Eyck. His proposal consisted of a series of cranking walls across the site that defined courtyards and through-routes as well as interior spaces. The layout of the walls encouraged future expansion in some places while limiting it in others in order to ensure a degree of spatial openness whatever the process of change. Van Eyck's drawings for the scheme are remarkable too, concentrating as much on the ephemeral realities of housing – washing lines, kids playing, neighbours chatting – as on their formal architectural character.

One of the revealing things about the PREVI scheme today is its relative obscurity in architectural terms. Given the stature of the architects involved, the project received little exposure and is not generally included in monographs of the practices' work. Van Eyck's scheme in particular – recognisable but substantially overlaid by modifications – remains a model for the framing of residents' involvement and the possibilities for dweller control.

Aldo van Eyck,
PREVI (Proyecto Experimental
de Vivienda),
Lima,
Peru,
1969

Van Eyck's scheme used diagonal single-storey walls to make twisting paths and public spaces between the houses and enclose small courtyard gardens. The competition organisers' decision to include a number of different architects' schemes across the overall site – rather than the one originally envisaged – meant that these spaces were more truncated and the routes less emphatic.

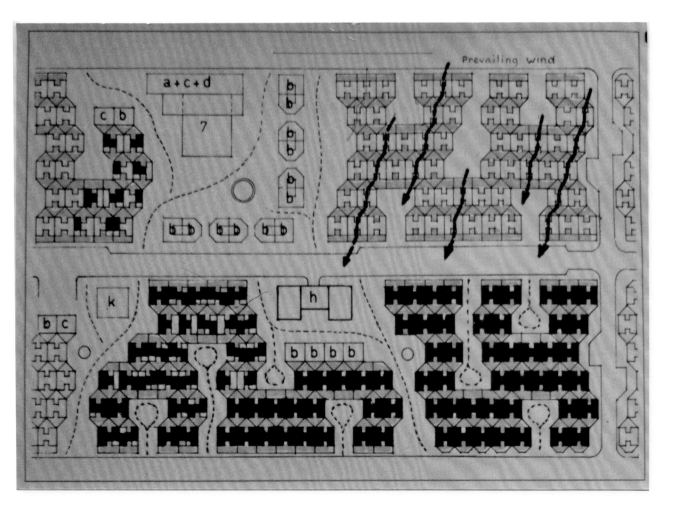

Aldo van Eyck,
PREVI (Proyecto
Experimental
de Vivienda),
Lima,
Peru,
1976

Van Eyck's spatial layout
employed a language of
courtyards and alleyways.
While the proposal encouraged
user adaptation, diagonal walls
were deployed to limit vertical
extensions where they might
harm the essential openness of
the courtyards.

Aldo van Eyck,
PREVI (Proyecto Experimental de Vivienda),
Lima,
Peru,
1980–82

The photographs show the process of resident modification over
time. Van Eyck's attempt to direct modification of certain areas of
the project was only partially successful.

Walters Way

The UK is notoriously averse to self-build, but there are sporadic examples worth studying. Some of the more interesting involve a system of timber-framed construction developed by the architect Walter Segal that allows relatively unskilled people to build their own homes.

The best known of these is Walters Way, a suburban close of detached houses built on a steep slope in Lewisham, London, in the mid-1980s and named after Segal himself. But there are numerous other examples, often on steep or otherwise hard to develop sites that do not suit traditional construction methods or forms of spatial planning.

The Diggers in Brighton, completed in 1996, is a good example of the legacy of Segal's methodology. Located on the edge of the city where it meets the South Downs, it is a collection of houses built by their occupants on a section of left-over land. In the process and design, the residents had the help of architects Archetype who updated Segal's method and principles.

The expressed timber structure and boxy appearance of the Diggers houses gives them a curious quality, appearing both modern and traditional at the same time. Their spatial arrangement is also interesting, with individual houses drifting casually down the slope in a way that eschews current obsessions with visual privacy and the rigid demarcation of private space. The space between the houses becomes an extension of the overall ethos, a relaxed and communal section of the hillside used for playing, gardening and socialising.

The Diggers,
Brighton,
UK,
1996

left: The houses employ a simple timber-frame construction system that allows them to be built on steeply sloping or otherwise inhospitable sites.

below: The landscape flows underneath and around individual dwellings. The usual demarcations of private and public realm are ignored and the landscape between the houses becomes occupied with tables, chairs, pots, plants and the informal jumble of outdoor domestic life.

Walter Segal,
Walters Way,
Lewisham,
London,
1980s

Walters Way is one of a number of self-build schemes in the London borough of Lewisham built in the 1970s and 1980s. The method of construction exploited sites the local council had not wanted to develop, allowing cooperatives of residents to build their own communities.

Oosterwold

Something similar is happening on a much larger scale in the new residential district of Oosterwold in Almere, the Netherlands. Almere itself has close to 200,000 residents and contains areas of custom and self-build housing where the state provides the infrastructure and residents do the rest. The results are a mixed bag, but the principle seems eminently sane with the state taking on the heavy lifting and residents gaining a level of freedom and creative input into their environment. Oosterwold is an even more extreme version of this process. Here residents group together to build their own sections of infrastructure – access roads, services and waterways – and 50 per cent of each plot has to be given over to 'urban farming'. Aside from dimensional restrictions governing boundaries and height, plot owners are free to build anything they want.

My practice is currently working on a house project in Oosterwold in collaboration with Invisible Studio. The early-stage proposals explore the relationship between the freedom of the architecture – anything goes within certain dimensional limits – and the very precise requirements for land use and the interface with neighbouring properties. Like the game Exquisite Corpse, the lines of road and pavement consistent from one plot to the next also allow an infinite inventiveness between. Far from being crude, the interplay of individual freedoms and collective responsibilities are subtle and interlinked.

Oosterwold,
Almere,
The Netherlands,
2017

The site is currently a cabbage field divided up into abstract rectangular plots. Each can be developed in its own way within strict regulations regarding land use, density and shared infrastructure requirements.

Shoreham-by-Sea,
West Sussex,
UK,
2016

In many ways a remnant of the spirit of 'Bungalow Town',
Shoreham's houseboats take on a spectacular variety of forms
and employ the detritus of more conventional forms of living.

The houseboats and the landscape around them are ongoing
projects, constantly subjected to a process of adding to and
modification where objects and materials may or may not be
used in future versions.

Bungalow New Town

A similar, related phenomenon occurred in the UK during the interwar years. Colin Ward has written about the 'plotland' settlements that developed in the southeast of England as a result of the early 20th-century agricultural depression.[2] These settlements were self-built and often linked to working-class communities escaping London life. They included extensive communities in Essex – especially in the area that is now Basildon New Town – as well as coastal settlements on Canvey Island and Jaywick Sands.

In Shoreham-by-Sea in West Sussex, though, a very particular community evolved out of a 'plotland' experiment. For a variety of reasons, 'Bungalow Town' – as it became known – grew up on the Shoreham seafront as the unofficial home of the early British film industry.[3] Actors, actresses and directors as well as others associated with the production of early silent movies built homes there. The films were made there too, using a large glazed building that took advantage of the natural light to film in.

Contemporary photographs of Bungalow Town show a remarkable collection of houses, elaborate confections that evoked castles, medieval cottages and maritime vessels. Whether the seemingly unconstrained creativity was a result of the fantasy of filmmaking or the freedom to construct your own home is unclear. The houses were cleared by the Ministry of Defence during the Second World War, ostensibly due to the need to make sea defences, but no doubt also because they and their eccentric community had never been popular with other locals. Besides, the movie industry had moved on. Take a walk along the muddy river's edge at Shoreham-by-Sea today, though, and you will still see a remarkable series of houseboats, each one an exercise in surreal bricolage and inventive DIY design. Buses, bathtubs, garden sheds, strange assemblages of fibreglass, bent plywood and just about any conceivable material have been used to make an extraordinary domestic landscape. Marginal it might be, but it demonstrates the vitality and creativity of self-built housing. ᴆ

Notes
1. Colin Ward, 'Until We Build Again', *Talking Houses: 10 Lectures*, Freedom Press (London), 1990, p 61.
2. Colin Ward, 'The Do-It-Yourself New Town', in *ibid*, pp 25–35.
3. NEB Wolters, *Bungalow Town: Theatre and Film Colony*, NEB Wolters (Shoreham-by-Sea), 1985.

Marginal it might be, but it demonstrates the vitality and creativity of self-built housing.

Cultivating Spaces to Take Risks

An Interview with Kate Goodwin, Drue Heinz Curator of Architecture at the Royal Academy of Arts

Kate Goodwin

Pezo von Ellrichshausen,
*Sensing Spaces:
Architecture Reimagined*,
Royal Academy of Arts,
London,
2014

Kate Goodwin: 'The intention
of *Sensing Spaces* was not to
create isolated installations, but to
choreograph an overall architectural
experience within a gallery and
exhibition context. As well as making
many formal propositions, this
particular installation highlighted
the sensations of vertical movement
through spiral staircases and a ramp
contained within it.'

A 250-year history does not stop London's Royal Academy of Arts from constantly exploring new ground. Its expanding architecture programme, led by Head of Architecture and Drue Heinz Curator **Kate Goodwin**, is no exception. Here she talks to Guest-Editor **Owen Hopkins** about the purposes and methods of cultural commissioning, and the curator's responsibilities to artists/ architects and public. Key to her approach are establishing mutual trust, resisting the temptation to play it safe, and knowing when to take a step back.

Recent years have seen a proliferation of exhibitions, debates, pavilions, projects of almost every kind, and even whole biennales geared towards architecture and exploring its place in the world.[1] At the same time, an increasing number of cultural institutions are incorporating architecture into their programmes, or rethinking, refocusing and expanding their existing offerings. In London there are now significant programmes being run by the Victoria and Albert Museum (V&A), the Design Museum, the Royal Institute of British Architects (RIBA), the Architecture Foundation and the Royal Academy of Arts (RA), among others. Founded in 1768, the RA is the oldest of all these institutions, and has had architects among its members since the beginning. Over the last three decades it has established a respected architecture programme as a means 'to present and encounter ideas' through a range of media including 'events, exhibitions, ideas competitions, awards, publications and commissions'. This has provided the bedrock for a number of notable, if irregularly scheduled, architecture exhibitions: from 'New Architecture: Foster, Rogers, Stirling' in 1986 to 2014's 'Sensing Spaces: Architecture Reimagined'. The latter was curated by the RA's Head of Architecture, Kate Goodwin, who is now in the process of overseeing an expansion of the institution's programmes in an attempt to establish its newly enlarged campus as a 'home for architecture' in London and beyond.

Given the way the Internet has decimated architectural journalism, and the increasing marketisation of academia, it is legitimate to ask whether the locus of architectural debate and new thinking has shifted to the sphere of curating and 'cultural commissions' in the form of pavilions or installations. This question becomes ever more pertinent when we acknowledge the fact that, while in some instances architectural programming has been aping other media in entering the realms of art, theatre and performance,[2] it does seemingly reflect a broadening appetite for and interest in architecture.

At the same time, the rise of the cultural commission also reflects changes in the commissioning of buildings and architectural patronage, and a consequent lack of opportunities – especially for younger architects – to be innovative. To make just one instructive comparison in how things have changed over recent decades: the competition for the Pompidou Centre, which attracted 681 competitors from 49 different countries, was eventually won by a young, inexperienced team with a genuinely radical design; versus the recent and wholly predictable shortlist of established global practices for London's proposed new concert hall. Moreover, that the Serpentine Gallery has, even with the stipulation that architects of its annual pavilion cannot have built in the UK before, been able to roll out such a roster of global stars to design it, is surely a damning indictment of the commissioning culture and regulatory systems that demand architects have a track record in a particular sector in order to bid for publicly funded projects.[3]

Diébédo Francis Kéré,
Serpentine Pavilion,
London,
2017

Kate Goodwin: 'Three years after *Sensing Spaces*, Kéré was invited to do the Serpentine Pavilion commission. Both works are about bringing people together, but in his Royal Academy installation he did so by encouraging audience interaction within the choreography of the exhibition, while in the pavilion he created a beautiful standalone structure that was an attractor in the landscape.'

Grafton Architects,
Sensing Spaces,
Royal Academy of Arts,
London,
2014

'Grafton's installation in many ways drew upon architecture, but also borrowed from theatre practice with a shifting light sequence that highlighted the profound impact of light upon our experience of architecture. It was much more than the creation of a structure, pushing them and myself into new and more risky territory that was ultimately very rewarding.'

Degrees of Freedom

However, the pavilion is not just an opportunity to build, but to experiment and work in a way that is distinct from normal ways of operating. And these types of commissions can also take place within gallery spaces. The most notable example of recent years was Goodwin's 'Sensing Spaces' exhibition, for which she took the bold step of commissioning seven different architects to create installations in the RA's neoclassical galleries 'to see if we could use "architecture" or architectural installations as a way to communicate about the complexity of our experience of architecture and the ways in which this can be powerful, especially when attuned to the body and senses'. While part of the brief was, Goodwin notes, 'about dealing with the architecture of the gallery and the exhibition experience', in terms of offering architects a different way of working there was much in common with the pavilion: 'Commissions give space for architects to act for a patron, to explore ideas they wouldn't otherwise have the opportunity to do.' As far as the prevalence of pavilion-type cultural commissions relates to external changes in how architects get work, she continues: 'If this was widespread practice for the procuring of architecture, then perhaps the pavilion wouldn't be as interesting. Regardless, I think there is always value in exploring the role of patronage and commissioning outside of the normal processes.'

If the phenomenon of the 'curator as commissioner' is a critique of the restrictions that govern how architects are typically forced to work, then for Goodwin at least it is only an implicit one. Yet the absence of normal constraints can be challenging in itself. 'What emerged from the conversations with a couple of the architects especially during the development stages of "Sensing Spaces" was that they found the freedom of the brief quite difficult, because constraints – planning regulations, function, operation, climate, site, urban context – were most often the starting point for designing the things they worked with and against; the tools that they needed. The relative absence of those things made it more difficult for them, but ultimately it pushed them into thinking in a different way and offered a freedom of thought that was very rewarding.'

But while a cultural commission might free architects from the constraints and demands within which they are used to working, the context of an exhibition – whether a pavilion, installation or a more conventional display – comes with its own set of conditions: 'There are a whole different series of things to work with: 2D, 3D, atmosphere, sound, relationship between objects and texts, and various ways in which those things come together; for example, you can put your work in relationship to another object or artwork.' Architects are also never free of budgetary considerations, and of the brief, here defined by the curator, who, depending on the nature of the exhibition may take a more leading role in shaping it in terms of content and even character, with the architect acting more akin to an exhibition designer. For Goodwin, however, the critical thing is that an exhibition 'spatialises ideas', communicating them to people in a way that is not possible through any other medium. Indeed, as a testing ground for new thinking, an exhibition might very reasonably be considered a failure unless those ideas successfully reach a target audience, if not the broader public, which is one of the fundamental distinctions between curating and academia.

'What emerged from the conversations with a couple of the architects especially during the development stages of "Sensing Spaces" was that they found the freedom of the brief quite difficult.'

Kengo Kuma,
Sensing Spaces,
Royal Academy of Arts,
London,
2014

'Kuma commonly uses installations as sites to experiment with new ideas, materials and making that he later uses in architectural work. In *Sensing Spaces*, he filled two rooms with scented bamboo connected with tiny plastic sleeves to create two opposing sensorial experiences: one within, the other outside of the delicate structure.'

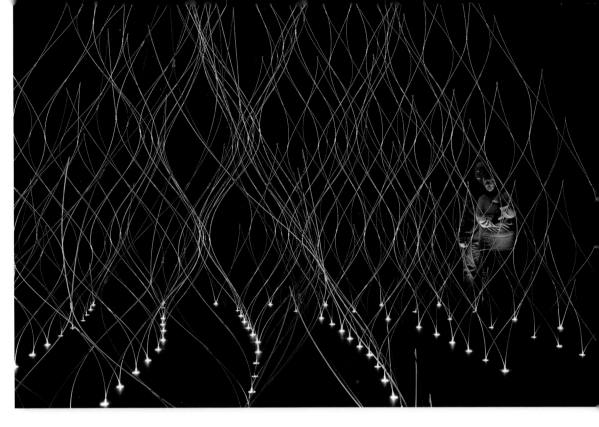

Diébédo Francis Kéré,
Sensing Spaces,
Royal Academy of Arts,
London, 2014

'Each work was in equal measure about a relationship with the 19th-century Beaux Arts galleries, the other installations and its own intentions. Kéré's installation invited the audience to populate the honeycomb plastic panels with straws, soon transforming it into a colourful hairy structure that created audible excitement in the process.'

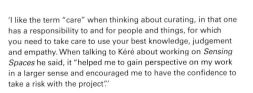

'I like the term "care" when thinking about curating, in that one has a responsibility to and for people and things, for which you need to take care to use your best knowledge, judgement and empathy. When talking to Kéré about working on *Sensing Spaces* he said, it "helped me to gain perspective on my work in a larger sense and encouraged me to have the confidence to take a risk with the project".'

Modes of Curating

On one level, the importance of communication brings the practice of curating in relation to journalism – both conceptually and professionally. One of the backdrops – and perhaps one of the driving forces – of the increased prominence of curating has been the structural changes in the publishing industry, particularly the trade press, with many curators of architecture refugees from journalism, as the opportunities and influence of that industry recede. Despite the superficiality of the similarities and equivalences between curating and journalism, the appearance of the journalist-curator has definitely affected approaches to architectural programming, and certainly in London. The V&A's 'Rapid Response Collecting' initiative, in which 'objects are collected in response to major moments in history that touch the world of design and manufacturing' – such as a 3D-printed gun, a pair of trousers manufactured in a factory in Bangladesh that collapsed in 2013, or just recently a TV-shirt designed for Jeremy Corbyn's general election campaign with a 'bootlegged' version of Nike's trademark swoosh – is clearly born out of a journalistic sensibility.[4] Elsewhere, much of the Architecture Foundation's programme has seemingly filled the critical and campaigning position that the trade press once occupied (unsurprising given it is in that field that its directors made their names).

As the practice of curating architecture has expanded, the identity of the curator has long lost its specificity in referring to those who look after collections. At the same time, looking beyond the realms of architecture the term has become increasingly debased as it is co-opted and used in all manner of fields: whether one is staging a restaurant experience, or even simply organising one's selfies on Instagram. This is, as Goodwin notes, 'to give a sense of authority, to give a sense that there is thought behind something, or that there's an integrity of thought'. Yet its etymology remains important and makes the distinction with journalism clear: 'The origins of the word "curating" go back to "care". And it was often caring for a collection. There's been a rise in collecting architecture, which I think is something that's important to interrogate, and might again challenge the current fluffy use of the term.'

'Inside Heatherwick Studio'
National Design Centre, Singapore, 2015

Kate Goodwin: 'In contrast to commissioning a new structure, architecture exhibitions provide the opportunity to expose the design process, which is often nonlinear and exploratory and therefore uncertain. I think that architecture requires clients to invest in the process and by revealing it within an exhibition, hope to encourage a spirit of patronage and show the creative value of the architect.'

'You're asking them to expose something about their process, something that they might not always be comfortable to do, and you do have a responsibility to that person.'

SO? Architecture and Ideas, *Unexpected Hill*, Royal Academy of Arts, London, 2016

'An important part of the curator's role is making finely balanced judgements that take into consideration all the parties that they have a responsibility to: the architect, funder – in this case Turkishceramics – the institution they represent and the audience. The audience is of particular concern for a commission like this where the intervention is in the public realm and there are significant health and safety implications. One needs to have the courage to take calculated risks that will enable a project to achieve something special.'

But for curators more typically engaged in programming, rather than in a particular collection, the idea of care takes on a different meaning, pointing to an aspect of the relationship between the curator and the architect(s) whose work they are curating. In this sphere it makes more sense to think of care in terms of the curator's 'responsibility' and where and to whom it lies. The responsibility of the architect is a well-rehearsed topic: their contractual and legal responsibilities to the client and building regulations, and also the more nebulous responsibility to society and the environment. The responsibility of the curator, in contrast, is far less clearly defined. Do or should those involved in curating architecture take a cue from architects' public mission, which some still see as distinguishing their practice from professions in the building construction industry? Or do the curator's responsibilities lie in relation to their institution or organisation, or those sponsoring their work? Should they be responsible to the architect they are commissioning, or to the profession more broadly, in selecting the right practitioner for what can be a transformative opportunity in terms of the platform the commission offers them?

As Goodwin implies, there is no single answer. On the one hand, the curator's responsibility 'is ultimately to your audience – both those who experience the work, but perhaps also those to whom the ideas may be disseminated through other means', and here that responsibility is largely to do with identifying the right work and architect to exhibit. Yet, on the other hand, as a curator commissioning an architect 'you are establishing the context and conditions in which you are asking them to operate. You are the person who connects that architect, that architectural thought, to the audience.' And in contrast to a client, in some cases the curator is asking an architect to be judged not by a finished building, but by the ideas from which it emerged, with the responsibility of ensuring that those ideas are presented and communicated in the best way. 'You're asking them to expose something about their process, something that they might not always be comfortable to do, and you do have a responsibility to that person to mediate that relationship, to take it forward, to frame it in a way that won't be misread or unjustly critiqued. And so I think there are quite a lot of responsibilities in that, but I also see it as a responsibility that's anchored in care and enabling somebody to take risks.'

Frank Kent and Jonathan Kipps,
Arches with Velvet Curtains,
Mayfair Art Weekend,
London,
2017

below and right: Kate Goodwin: 'My role at the Royal Academy has also involved commissioning artists, which has been a very good lesson. When operating in a field that I know less about my judgement is strongly guided by instinct. This results in the setting of an exciting brief, bringing my spatial skills to the conversation and then stepping back and allowing the artist to have the freedom to come up with something that I could not begin to conceive.'

'I have found the most successful relationships and outcomes have been those where there has been a strong dialogue.'

However, a key part of the role is also knowing when and where to step back. 'If you're asking an architect to come up with an idea, to push it, it should be their own. You need to set a framework in which they can think and respond, but you also need to know where to step in and step out.' In contrast to the architect–client relationship, the critical role of the curator is not about creating a brief (although that is part of it), but in 'cultivating the space for them to generate their idea and take risks. To my mind, it's about enabling them to create something that they might not have been able to do within the context where they generally operate.' In this way, the freedom a cultural project offers an architect is not just through loosening the usual constraints they work within, but having a curator who carries some of the creative risk and allows them to take a 'leap of faith in the knowledge that the groundwork is there, that the project will be delivered, that the parameters are being set down right, that the vision is right'.

Grafton Architects,
Sensing Spaces development workshop,
Royal Academy of Arts,
London,
2013

'My relationship and involvement with each of the architects involved in *Sensing Spaces* varied. With Yvonne Farrell and Shelley McNamara of Grafton Architects, I had an extended creative and intellectual dialogue that informed the shape of the exhibition and the development of their specific response. I find that building trust and understanding is vital when commissioning, as it enables both the curator and architects to take risks.'

Risks and Rewards

Alongside the opportunities for creative experimentation and media and public exposure that cultural commissions offer those architects who take part in them, there is the danger that as a type they end up promoting a very particular idea of what architecture is or should be – essentially architecture and architectural ideas that are readily communicable. Moreover, for curators working in institutional settings there can be requirements to hit audience targets that can create internal pressure for work that is spectacular, crowd-pleasing, and by already established 'big names'. The Serpentine Pavilion is the most notable example of this tendency, a project that when first established was genuinely radical, but which, notwithstanding some interesting individual pavilions, as an endeavour has become stale and predictable. Moreover, its emphasis on 'architecture-as-sculpture' appears a world away from the more mundane though vital concerns that architecture should ultimately be wrestling with.

Like the cultural commission itself, the relationship between curator and architect is essentially paradoxical. While the curator offers the architect a space to work in that is to a large extent free of the constraints that usually govern their practice, that space comes with its own set of both practical and intellectual considerations. In a world where architects are typically used to trying to find ways of expanding or maximising their agency, the curator is asking architects to voluntarily give up some of their agency and share it with them. For Goodwin, it is ultimately about trust – and trust that works both ways. 'It's about respecting the architects, understanding how they work, and what motivates them. I have found the most successful relationships and outcomes have been those where there has been a strong dialogue that doesn't take anything for granted, but opens new spaces of thought and creativity for both of us. There is also something very important about knowing when to let go and trust – trust that you have set the vision clearly enough and that they can take it on and create something unexpected. There have been moments when the architects (and also artists) have had visions or ideas that I couldn't immediately see but have trusted none-the-less, and the result has been incredible – it's the reason for working with other people.' ◬

This article is based on a conversation between Owen Hopkins and Kate Goodwin at the Royal Academy of Arts, London, in September 2017.

Notes
1. Examples of biennales include the Chicago Architecture Biennial (founded in 2015), Istanbul Design Biennial (established 2012), and the Tallinn Architecture Biennial (established 2011).
2. Examples include the Storefront for Art and Architecture in New York, some of the activities of Raven Row gallery in London, and even some of the recent installations at the RIBA, such as *The Brutalist Playground* (2015) by Assemble and artist Simon Terrill, and *We Live in the Office* (2016–17), a commission by artist Giles Round.
3. For more information on current trends, see the report by Walter Menteth, *A Synopsis of UK Architectural Competitions Practices and Trends*, Project Compass CIC, 2017: https://researchportal.port.ac.uk/portal/files/6727925/17_03_05_PC_Report_AL_UK_Procurement_R2_Final.pdf.
4. As described on the V&A's website: www.vam.ac.uk/blog/tag/rapid-response-collecting.

Shared Memories of a Possible Future

An Interview with Umbrellium's Usman Haque

Usman Haque

Umbrellium,
Open Burble,
Singapore Biennale,
2006

The Burble has appeared in various incarnations
over its history. The Mini Burble, for example,
is a 10-storey mobile structure made of 300
large balloons that form a nimble and reactive
structure that visitors are able to 'paint' on.
Each balloon contains sensors, LEDs and
microcontrollers enabling the balloons to create
patterns of colour rippling skyward. Once
it is launched, members of the public use a
Mini Burble App to paint the colours that flow
through the 30-metre (98-foot) form.

Owen Hopkins

Usman Haque's practice is not what you would immediately think of as architecture. But, as founding partner of London-based urban technology designers Umbrellium, Haque is having an impact in areas associated with the discipline. As he reveals here in conversation with Guest-Editor **Owen Hopkins**, he is particularly concerned with empowering ordinary people to take part in decision-making processes about the creation of their living environment.

The work of Usman Haque defies conventional categorisation. His projects at Umbrellium, which was previously Haque Design + Research, encompass everything from software for public space and participatory cultural infrastructure, to an augmented reality app for visualising real-time environmental data and a search engine for the Internet of Things, and much else besides. On the surface, these projects seem far from the traditional domain of architecture. Yet unifying them all is a deeply held belief in using technology to empower people both on an individual and societal level, and to engage them in decision-making around the future of cities – an endeavour that many architects would have great sympathy with, even if they look to achieve it through rather different means. Indeed, Haque himself sees his work as 'intentionally architectural': 'My desire is to contribute to the debate about the discipline of architecture, more so than technology or design or even as an artist. The discipline I want to contribute to and affect some change in is architecture.'

However, when it comes to matters of the changing status and extent of that discipline – and the challenges that poses to architects' agency – with which this issue of 𝐃 is concerned, Haque turns the question around: 'When I talk about crisis of agency, I'm actually talking about ordinary people with respect to decision-making in cities, rather than the crisis of agency of the architect.' For him, this crisis stems from a disconnect between the city and its inhabitants: 'There's a sense that the city is separate from us, that the city is some structures that we inhabit, and that somehow we are temporary occupants of something that's provided to us to exist in for the duration that we're there.' A key part of the reason for this, Haque believes, is that people are excluded from making fundamental decisions about where they live, with the corollary that 'by not making decisions, you almost fall out of any ongoing responsibility for outcomes or the future of the city'.

'My desire is to contribute to the debate about the discipline of architecture, more so than technology or design or even as an artist. The discipline I want to contribute to and affect some change in is architecture.'

Umbrellium,
VoiceOver,
Horden,
County Durham,
2016

above: VoiceOver is an urban-scale communication infrastructure that forms a chain of interactive light and sound that everyone can listen in on, and whose spectacular luminescent path depends on residents who choose to host a network node.

A Prisoner's Dilemma

Each of Haque's projects, therefore, aims to actively engage people in the decision-making processes that they are more used to being excluded from, and in doing so break the cycle that locks them into what he sees as a kind of 'prisoner's dilemma' of inaction and disempowerment: 'I'm trying to invert all of that, and figure out at every step how I can open up what I do as the designer of a system – or as an architect – to allow more and more decisions to be taken on by others, not for the sake of it, but to build in from the beginning the fact that the outcome of the project is a sense of agency and responsibility by the people who are involved in it.' This is an intriguing point, because it is not simply saying that the project is all about the process, as has become voguish for some architects to suggest, but that the physical outcome is a means of realising a broader social one. 'Some projects might have blinking lights, or some projects might have augmented reality, or some other projects might have plants or physical structure, but really the outcome is not these manifestations, it is more importantly the sense of accomplishment, responsibility and decision-making that binds people together into something we could call a community.'

Even if we assume that on some level the crisis of agency among people in cities is nothing new, and has perhaps existed as long as cities themselves, it is, Haque suggests, more urgent now than at any previous moment. Part of this is simply scale: 'The sheer numbers of interactions between people and with our environment have very complex consequences that are nonlinear and unpredictable.' But also: 'Our capacity now, even as small groups of individuals, to affect things going on on the other side of the planet is greater than before. I mean that both in an environmental sense, but also in terms of our decisions to purchase stuff that is cheap, that happens, for example, to be built in China, that has its own kind of social-political context and reasons for which things are cheap.' 'Technology', Haque points out, 'is at the intersection of all of this. The pace of change now means that if we are not more consciously making decisions about technology as groups of people, the consequences are greater than ever before.'

Umbrellium,
Thingful,
2013–

right: Thingful is a search engine for the Internet of Things, providing a unique geographical index of connected objects around the world, including energy, radiation, weather and air-quality devices as well as seismographs, iBeacons, ships, aircraft and even animal trackers.

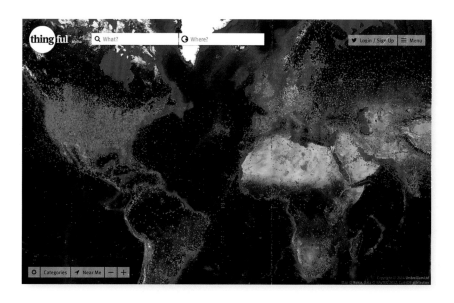

'It's all about peoples'
relationship to each other,
to the environment
around them.'

Umbrellium,
Assemblance,
London,
2014

A challenge in today's dynamic urban
environments is to develop interfaces that
enable collaborative design, building and
reconfiguration of space on the fly through
responsive technologies. The aim of
Assemblance, a fully immersive interactive
augmented-reality environment made
'real' by using light as a physical material,
is to structure participation and build trust
between people who must sometimes
suspend disbelief in order to cooperate
and coexist.

Umbrellium,
Linguine,
Bradford,
West Yorkshire,
2012

above: Linguine is a software platform Umbrellium has developed to make it easy to design and deploy citizen-focused interactive environments in public urban spaces. With Linguine, all stages of the production process use the same piece of software, allowing a continuity of medium through which ongoing, iterative design feedback is possible – even after the space has been occupied – to enable a better design process and continual design improvements.

Shared Contexts

At first glance, architecture seems irrelevant to much of this. Yet the question as to how technology is applied – and its inherent capacity to be continually 're-scripted', as Haque sees it – does have significant ramifications for architecture. For Haque, it again comes down to decision-making – not just who makes those decisions, but how they are made. 'It cascades up to anyone involved in the design of systems: how do they make decisions about what they are doing in such a way that they leave sufficient decision-making capacity for those people who are actually going to be affected by what they're doing to be invested enough in it to see a positive and sustainable outcome?' It is a convoluted question, but a vital one.

When asked about whether he sees what he is doing as a model that other architects could or should adopt, Haque concedes that in comparison to even two decades ago many architects now 'at the very least pay lip service to this and in most cases deliver on a people-centric approach'. However, he is quick to point out that while this is positive development, it is not just about 'saying we are people-centric', but 'having a deep understanding of the complexity of the context you're about to embark on working in', and vitally, ensuring that 'there is a shared understanding between all of the project partners. The starting point has to be about getting a shared perspective; to get a shared memory of a possible future; to get everyone understanding the complexity, understanding the potential risk.' The latter point is another vital one for architecture, with fear and mitigation of financial and creative 'risk' so often holding back innovation. By binding all interested parties together into the decision-making process, the potential for blame to be apportioned to one individual or group is therefore minimised, if not entirely removed.

Bringing the conversation back to where we started, given the challenge Haque's approach poses to conventional practice, does it make sense to still describe it as architecture? His response is unequivocal: 'I'm not that concerned about nomenclature, but in order to give shape to what I'm doing I am quite proud of the concept of architecture. It's all about people's relationship to each other, to the environment around them, and to the question of their own self-determination and futures in those environments.' Architects take note. ∆

This article is based on a telephone conversation between Owen Hopkins and Usman Haque in August 2017.

Umbrellium,
Natural Fuse,
2011–

Natural Fuse is a microscale CO_2 monitoring and overload protection framework that works locally and globally, harnessing the carbon-sinking capabilities of plants. A power socket enables people to power or recharge their electrical appliances and devices while the plant's growth offsets the carbon footprint of the energy expended. Since typical energy use requires more than one plant to offset an appliance's carbon footprint, Natural Fuses are networked so that unused carbon offsetting capacity in the network as a whole can be accounted for as necessary.

The Omniscience and Dependency of Practice

COUNTERPOINT
03/2018
No 253

The function of and need for architects is constantly being called into question – not least in this issue of 𝝙. So what is their relevance in this world of self-build, prefabrication, digitalisation and the primacy of capital? Architect and technologist **Phil Bernstein**, who teaches at Yale University, offers his vision of the practical steps needed for them to secure the agency that constitutes professional freedom, while fully living up to their ethical and societal responsibilities.

'Coach, Husband, Architect, Father. One Title Was Fake' was the surprising headline in a recent edition of the *New York Times*.[1] It seems that one Paul Newman (only acting as an architect, no relation) had been practising architecture in upstate New York under a stolen license number and fake seal. He was sentenced to seven years in prison for, among other things, defrauding his clients of $200,000 in fees. 'So what?', decried Aaron Betsky in *Architect* magazine,[2] who wondered if Newman had really done anything wrong. His buildings seemed reasonable, building officials approved his plans for permit, and nothing he designed fell down, caught fire or otherwise injured an unsuspecting public. That he lacked proper professional credentials was somehow beside the point, as it seemed that his alleged 'competency' was a low enough bar. Betsky went on to make the argument that, given the typical mediocrity of most buildings designed by those properly credentialled, licensure signals nothing meaningful since it rarely assures 'good architecture'.

Existential Threats

As I have argued elsewhere,[3] Betsky's conclusions present an existential threat to the profession, since without the foothold of licensure, clients would opt out of using architects altogether. But I suspect that, with few exceptions (Patrik Schumacher, Jo Noero), most of the contributors to this edition of 𝝙 would be completely sympathetic to his stance, privileging the remit of the architect to produce good architecture as purely an aesthetic and/or ethical enterprise, and in some cases exclusively so. That our profession has these obligations is without question, and I dare say most of us entered it with aspirations to create good architecture in some form. But asking whether the discipline and the profession have

Grenfell Tower,
London,
June 2017

Multiple systemic failures
to protect the public's
health, safety and welfare
resulted in the deaths of at
least 80 people.

the freedom to achieve these lofty goals without an examination of means versus ends – and in particular, the architect as a professional participant in the systems of delivery – is a bit like admiring a Formula One race and omitting any consideration of track conditions, driver skills or even the design of the cars themselves.

Several of the essays in this issue question whether we need architects at all (Adam Nathaniel Furman), or whether architecture demands clients in any traditional sense (Kata Fodor, Anupama Kundoo, Sarah Wigglesworth). Others offer the primary agency of design to users (Usman Haque), or demand the autonomy of expression beyond buildings (Furman) or the autonomy of the dweller (Charles Holland). The internal mechanisms of practice abuse the worker in the service of the creative endeavour as the neoliberal economy turns architects into automatons of the system (Peggy Deamer). The resources of architecture are either beyond the architect's control, or even responsibility, and in almost every case work against the grander aspirations by inhibiting the freedom of architects to do the right thing.

Systems of Accountability

Unless making architecture is purely a conjectural or theoretical exercise, our work must be actualised as real, physical things that occupy space, require money, consume resources, meet safety and regulatory constraints, and fulfil the needs of the clients who commissioned them. In the modern world, society has sanctioned a credentialled professional – an architect – to be responsible, and defined his or her agency in specific ways. This is not a hypothetical assertion: modern humans inhabit buildings a vast majority of their days, and disasters like the collapse of the Hotel New World

in Singapore in 1986 or the Kansas City Hyatt Regency bridge disintegration in 1981 demonstrate both the need for health and safety certification and structures of responsibility to hold the system accountable. The recent fire at Grenfell Tower in London, now swirling in recrimination for exactly who might have been responsible, suggests that the systems of delivery do not, in and of themselves, assure the safety of the public.

Perhaps we might examine the concept of 'freedom' as a function of that professional agency within systems of capital, materials, regulations and use in an effort to exercise that very potent weapon in the service of good architecture. You either understand, navigate and manipulate the system, or it manipulates you. And, as suggested above, those systems may fail disastrously without accountability.

Do We Need Architects?

The bland assertion that architects are not 'needed' is easily defended from the vantage point of those systems of delivery – the economic, technical and legal constructs within which the built environment is actualised. The deterioration of the architect's responsibilities for design, most vividly exemplified by the emergence of the subdiscipline of contracting called 'design management', or even our continuing separation from the means and methods of construction, could be read as troubling signs of our impending irrelevance. I am writing this essay from Singapore, where a government-sponsored initiative to improve construction called 'integrated digital delivery' includes the automated manufacture of large building components (facades, toilets, even entire apartment units), forcing architects to incorporate major standardised building elements like we once specified doorknobs. Not much freedom

Singapore skyline,
2011

Recent attempts at improved
design have mostly come from
international architects, for
example Moshe Safdie's Marina
Bay Sands resort, seen on the
left of the photo.

Architects need the freedom
– dare I say power – to control
building if architecture is a means
for establishing and articulating
social order ... aesthetic meaning
and relevance ... or the ethical
freedom of use.

to make good architecture coming from there, I'm afraid, but a bellwether of delivery methodology to come. In a place where 90 per cent of the population lives in public housing designed and delivered by the state, there is nary a mention of – nor interest in – aesthetic or ethical considerations that might yield good architecture. In fact, the 'designed' buildings of Singapore have mostly been delivered by the private sector hiring outside architects.

In the US, a surge of interest in prefabrication is putting additional pressure on architects to fit the mould. Companies specialising in modular construction, which make claims to have premanufactured buildings erected and 'dried in' (protected from the weather) in less than 20 days, are optimising something other than design and only feign interest in good architecture. As building moves inevitably towards such mass customisation, degrees of architectural independence will suffer accordingly.

Architects need the freedom – dare I say power – to control building if architecture is a means for establishing and articulating social order (Schumacher), aesthetic meaning and relevance (Furman) or the ethical freedom of use (Noero). Theoretical speculation about that agency (even if it may often verge on whinging, as has been the case during my entire multi-decade career) may be aspirational or inspirational, but often misses the central issue: good architecture is only produced by architects in positions of professional efficacy. Redefining architecture's role in the neoliberal economy is, beyond speculation, way above our professional pay grade, and barring a raft of architects taking high office we must work from the perches we are granted.

Gluck+,
The Stack,
New York,
2016

A prefabricated, seven-storey apartment building by an integrated architect-led firm that designed both the building and the process by which it was constructed.

Levers of Power and Influence

Access to those perches will be granted from three sources: clients, regulatory systems and delivery economics. First and most influential are the people who hire architects to make actual buildings for real purposes and who set the constraints of our agency. The disconnect between the interests of clients and good architecture in whatever form are partially a function of our inability to demonstrate to those clients that our agendas, recommendations and resulting design solutions are in the larger social interest. We choose to privilege spatial and expressive outcomes, but many buildings (though not all) have higher aspirations: hospitals to improve health, or schools to educate. If we want the agency to promise such ends, we will need to demonstrate that our work achieves them. If the ends are not of interest to the architect, then he or she should refuse the commission. In either case, is that not 'good design' in its most ethical sense?

Demonstrations, rather than mere speculations, of good architecture during design itself would go far in building the credibility of architects and result immediately in augmented influence should we choose to actually commit to the outcomes that we often assert are the result of good building. Technology provides ample opportunity to predict building characteristics or performance, spatially or technically. Large-scale data gathering during construction to understand design efficacy, or during building use to collect and evaluate the actual impacts of projects in operation as functional, occupied artefacts – and then sharing the resulting insights amongst us – could substantiate our arguments that our buildings actually do important things.

Architects are empowered by systems of regulation by the requirement that we participate in the design and construction of a building to assure public welfare. Today that responsibility is defined in the narrowest sense – life safety. But what if 'public welfare' was as expansive a concept as is suggested in the various essays in this volume, yet with the force of legal authority behind it, actuated by architects themselves? If today our lever of influence is public safety in its most limited sense, perhaps we should make the case that public welfare itself includes consideration of spatial expression, social advancement, environmental responsibility, even livable cities. If that list, which in our professional ethos is long, were in some form our legal remit then our freedom to create good architecture would expand accordingly.

There are strategies and implications of such an idea. Like many professions we create, manage and control the mechanisms of professional certification. Expanding our licensable remit would magnify our influence towards the good, but only if that remit were accompanied by a parallel increase in our willingness to take responsibility for the broadest definition of 'good architecture'.

Finally, while architects may have originated as 'master builders', today our relationship with building – and the complex flows of money, responsibilities, materials and labour it requires – is ambivalent at best. Digital modelling and fabrication are drawing those worlds closer as design information forms a more direct basis of construction instructions, particularly as building becomes more industrialised and automated and a new generation of firms explore the resulting design opportunities. In that sense, delivery is becoming design itself. Architects should create and manage the resulting protocols fully, as exchanges of valuable information and reducers of risk, so as to increase our agency in the heart of the delivery complex, putting us right in the centre of the key decisions that make architecture in its widest sense.

Alloy,
One John Street,
Brooklyn,
New York,
2016

This housing project was developed, designed, constructed and sold by Alloy, a firm of 18 architects who operate a self-contained delivery system where they have complete control, assume all the risk, and reap the resulting rewards.

Gramazio Kohler Research,
Mesh Mould,
DFAB House,
ETH Zurich,
2016–17

Aspects of construction will be automated at various scales, demonstrated by this on-site robot that welds concrete reinforcement in complex shapes in situ.

In a 2015 speculation, OMA/AMO's Reinier de Graaf contrasts two lenses of architecture: 'In economic terms it is a largely reactive discipline, a response to pre-formulated needs. In intellectual terms it is the opposite: a visionary domain that claims the future … [since] both conditions are equally true, architecture [is] a curious form of omniscience practiced in a context of utter dependency.'[4] He argues that architects are educated only in the visionary to the exclusion of any understanding of the context of practice itself, and the resulting 'Ignorance of this mechanism coupled with a misplaced hubris creates a lethal cocktail, in which the architect inevitably becomes complicit in the causes antithetical to the ones he claims to profess'.[5] The antidote to the resulting poison is actively participating in the platforms of practice, strengthening levers of influence like licensure, redesigning the flows of information, capital and risk that comprise delivery as architectural problems, defining the tools and instruments of design from software to contracts, and, as De Graaf suggests, having the freedom to 'play the system against itself' in the service of good architecture. ⌂

Notes
1. Michael Wilson, 'Coach, Husband, Architect, Father. One Title Was Fake', *New York Times*, 11 September 2017: www.nytimes.com/2017/09/11/nyregion/architect-fraud-vandelay-industries-paul-newman.html?_r=0.
2. Aaron Betsky, '"Architect" Goes to Jail, World Shrugs', *Architect*, 21 September 2017: www.architectmagazine.com/practice/architect-goes-to-jail-world-shrugs_o.
3. Phil Bernstein, 'Bernstein on Betsky', *Architect*, 4 October 2017: www.architectmagazine.com/practice/bernstein-on-betsky_o.
4. Reinier de Graaf, 'I Will Learn You Architecture!', *Volume*, 45, 16 October 2015: http://volumeproject.org/i-will-learn-you-architecture/.
5. *Ibid.*

Architects are educated only in the visionary to the exclusion of any understanding of the context of practice itself

CONTRIBUTORS

Phil Bernstein is an architect, technologist and educator. He teaches at Yale University where he received both his BA and his MArch. He was formerly a Vice-President at Autodesk where he was responsible for the company's future vision and strategy for technology for the building industry. Prior to this he was a principal with Pelli Clarke Pelli Architects. He is the co-author (with Peggy Deamer) of *Building (In) The Future: Recasting Labor in Architecture* (Princeton University Press, 2008) and *BIM In Academia* (Yale School of Architecture, 2011), and is currently writing a book on the future of practice and technology to be published by Birkhäuser in 2018.

Carlo Cappai and Maria Alessandra Segantini are the principals and directors of C+S Architects, based in Venice and London. Both graduated with honours from the IUAV in Venice, and are registered architects both in Italy and the UK. Their work has been exhibited at the Museum of Modern Art (MoMA) in New York, the 15th Venice Architecture Biennale and at the Massachusetts Institute of Technology (MIT) in Boston, where they are visiting professors. Awards include the Gold Medal of Italian Architecture 2012 special prize, In-Opera Award 2012, and the SFIDE 2009 Award of the Italian Ministry of the Environment. They have lectured internationally, including at Cornell and Columbia universities in New York, the Polytechnic University of Milan, Delft University of Technology, the École Polytechnique Fédérale de Lausanne (EPFL) in Switzerland, and Cambridge and Bath universities in the UK.

Peggy Deamer is Professor of Architecture at Yale University. She received a BArch from the Cooper Union in New York, and a PhD from Princeton University, New Jersey, and is a principal of the firm Deamer Architects. Her current research explores the relationship between subjectivity, design and labour in today's economy. She is the editor of *Architecture and Capitalism: 1845 to the Present* (Routledge, 2013) and *The Architect as Worker: Immaterial Labor, the Creative Class, and the Politics of Design* (Bloomsbury, 2015), and co-editor of *Asymmetric Labors: The Economy of Architecture in Theory and Practice* (The Architecture Lobby, 2016). She is the founding member of the Architecture Lobby, a group advocating for the value of architectural design and labour.

Kata Fodor graduated from the Royal Danish Academy of Fine Arts' Urbanism and Societal Change programme with a thesis project on reinventing the Frankfurt kitchen, before founding Atelier Kite, a multidisciplinary design studio. She works in Denmark, Ireland and the UK on research-driven design strategies. Affordable housing and sustainable urban food systems are her main interests. She also holds a BA from the Academy of Fine Arts Vienna, and previously worked for Viennese offices feld72 and querkraft.

Adam Nathaniel Furman is a London-based designer whose practice ranges from architecture and interiors to sculpture, installation, writing and product design. He pursues research through his studio Productive Exuberance at Central Saint Martins, and the research group Saturated Space, which he co-runs at the Architectural Association (AA). He has worked at OMA Rotterdam, Ron Arad Architects, Farrells and Ash Sakula, and has written for the *Architectural Review*, *RIBA Journal*, *Abitare*, *Icon* and *Apollo*, amongst others.

Kate Goodwin is Head of Architecture and Drue Heinz Curator at the Royal Academy of Arts, London, where she is responsible for both architecture exhibitions and programming activity. She curated the exhibition 'Sensing Spaces: Architecture Reimagined' (2014) at the Royal Academy, and 'New British Inventors: Inside Heatherwick Studio' for the British Council, which toured East Asia (2015–16). She oversees the Academy's creative programming and is on the Mayfair Art Weekend Board. She was awarded a Royal Institute of British Architects (RIBA) Honorary Fellowship in 2016 in recognition of her contribution to the profession.

Usman Haque is founding partner of Umbrellium and Thingful, a search engine for the Internet of Things. Trained as an architect, he has created responsive environments, interactive installations, digital interface devices and mass-participation initiatives throughout the world. His skills include the design and engineering of both physical spaces and the software and systems that bring them to life. He has also taught at the Bartlett School of Architecture, University College London (UCL). He received the 2008 Design of the Year Award (interactive) from the Design Museum, London, a 2009 World Technology Award (art), the Japan Media Arts Festival Excellence prize, and the Asia Digital Art Award Grand Prize.

Charles Holland is an architect, teacher and writer. He is the principal of Charles Holland Architects (CHA), a design and research practice. The firm's current work includes residential, civic and public art projects. He is also a Professor of Architecture at the University of Brighton, where his research focuses on housing and new settlements, particularly in 'ruburban' and rural settings. He writes and lectures about architecture and the work of his practice, and contributes a monthly column to the *RIBA Journal* on the subject of utopias.

Anupama Kundoo founded her architectural practice in 1990 in Auroville, India. She focuses on material research to achieve architecture of low environmental impact that is also socio-economically beneficial, and has experience of working, researching and teaching architecture in a variety of cultural contexts across the world. She graduated from the University of Mumbai in 1989, and completed her PhD at the Technical University of Berlin in 2008. She is currently based in Madrid. Her research-oriented practice has exhibited twice at the Venice Architecture Biennale, with *Feel the Ground. Wall House: One to One* in 2012, and *Building Knowledge: An Inventory of Strategies* in 2016.

Anna Minton is a Reader in Architecture at the University of East London, and also Programme Leader of its Master of Research course Reading the Neoliberal City. She is the author of *Big Capital: Who is London For?* (Penguin, 2017) and *Ground Control: Fear and Happiness in the Twenty-First-Century City* (Penguin, 2009). Between 2011 and 2014, she was the 1851 Royal Commission for the Great Exhibition Fellow in the Built Environment. She is a regular contributor to the *Guardian*, and a frequent broadcaster and conference speaker.

Jo Noero has been in practice since 1984. His firm's work has been recognised internationally through publications, awards and exhibitions including RIBA's Lubetkin Prize in 2006. He was elected an Honorary Fellow of the American Institute of Architects (AIA) in 2015, International Fellow of the RIBA in 2010, and also received the Gold Medal for Architecture from the South African Institute of Architects. He was Ruth and Norman Moore Professor and Director of Graduate Studies at Washington University in St Louis, Missouri, from 1995 to 2000. He was appointed Director of the School of Architecture and Planning at the University of Cape Town in 2000, where he was Professor of Architecture until 2014. He became Emeritus Professor in 2015.

Patrik Schumacher is principal of Zaha Hadid Architects and has led the firm since Zaha Hadid's passing in March 2016. He joined the practice in 1988. In 1996 he founded the Design Research Laboratory (DRL) at the AA, where he continues to teach. Over the last 20 years he has contributed over 100 articles to architectural journals and anthologies. Since 2007 he has been promoting 'parametricism' as an epochal style for the 21st century. He is the author of *The Autopoiesis of Architecture* (John Wiley & Sons, 2010/12), and Guest-Editor of △ *Parametricism 2.0: Rethinking Architecture's Agenda for the 21st Century* (March/April 2016), emphasising the societal relevance of the style.

Alex Scott-Whitby is the founding director of ScottWhitbyStudio, an award-winning architecture and urban design consultancy that works within, on and outside the boundaries of traditional architectural and urban design practice. He is currently admissions tutor and a senior lecturer at the University of East London, and has previously taught at the AA, the Welsh School of Architecture, and IUAV in Venice. In 2016 he led a multinational and transdisciplinary team to win the Unlimited Doha Design Prize, and was named by the *RIBA Journal* as one of the Rising Stars of British Architecture.

Ines Weizman is Professor of Architectural Theory, Director of the Bauhaus Institute for History and Theory of Architecture and Planning, and Director of the Centre for Documentary Architecture at the Bauhaus University in Weimar, Germany. She trained as an architect at the Bauhaus, École d'Architecture de Belleville in Paris, the Sorbonne, University of Cambridge and the AA, where she completed her PhD thesis. Her publications include *Architecture and the Paradox of Dissidence* (Routledge, 2014), and (with Eyal Weizman) *Before and After: Documenting the Architecture of Disaster* (Strelka Press, 2015). She also edited (with Jorge Otero-Pailos) the 'Preservation and Copyright' issue of the journal *Future Anterior*.

Sarah Wigglesworth is director of her London-based architectural practice, which she founded in 1994. She also teaches, writes and speaks about the built environment. Specialising in exploring sustainable futures, her practice has designed buildings for the educational, community, masterplanning, cultural and housing sectors, in particular specialist housing, and has won many awards. Her work has been published throughout the world and she is a sought-after speaker. In 2003 she was awarded an MBE for her services to architecture, and in 2012 was appointed a Royal Designer for Industry by the Royal Society for the Encouragement of Arts, Manufactures and Commerce (RSA).

What is Architectural Design?

Founded in 1930, *Architectural Design* (△) is an influential and prestigious publication. It combines the currency and topicality of a newsstand journal with the rigour and production qualities of a book. With an almost unrivalled reputation worldwide, it is consistently at the forefront of cultural thought and design.

Each title of △ is edited by an invited Guest-Editor, who is an international expert in the field. Renowned for being at the leading edge of design and new technologies, △ also covers themes as diverse as architectural history, the environment, interior design, landscape architecture and urban design.

Provocative and pioneering, △ inspires theoretical, creative and technological advances. It questions the outcome of technical innovations as well as the far-reaching social, cultural and environmental challenges that present themselves today.

For further information on △, subscriptions and purchasing single issues see:

http://onlinelibrary.wiley.com/journal/10.1002/%28ISSN%291554-2769

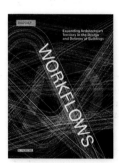

Volume 87 No 3
ISBN 978 1119 317845

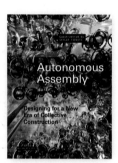

Volume 87 No 4
ISBN 978 1119 102359

Volume 87 No 5
ISBN 978 1119 152644

Volume 87 No 6
ISBN 978 1119 340188

Volume 88 No 1
ISBN 978 1119 379515

Volume 88 No 2
ISBN 978 1119 254416